Winged Leviathan

The Story of the Humpback Whale

Winged Leviathan

The Story of the Humpback Whale by Phil Clapham

Photographs by Colin Baxter

Colin Baxter Photography, Grantown-on-Spey, Scotland

Contents

Foreword

On the 16th of February 1973, in Southern Ocean waters some 1,200 miles south-southeast of the Cape of Good Hope, a catcher boat from the Soviet factory ship *Yuri Dolgorukiy* was pursuing a 13-m male humpback whale. As he had done innumerable times before, the harpooner on the bow took aim and fired as the whale surfaced in front of him. The huge steel harpoon shot through the air and crashed into the whale's side, igniting an explosive charge which probably killed the animal instantly.

With the death of that whale, a long and tragic history finally came to a close. For neither the catcher crew nor the whale could have known at the time that this would be the very last humpback to be killed by the commercial whaling industry, the final victim of a slaughter that had begun centuries before.

The whale's demise had been preceded by the deaths of literally hundreds of thousands of other humpbacks. Beginning sometime in the Middle Ages, men seeking profit from the whale's meat or oil-rich blubber had hunted and killed humpbacks, first in coastal waters using small sailing craft and hand-thrown harpoons; then, as technology improved, from large sailing ships; and finally from steam-powered catcher boats working from huge floating factory ships that relentlessly pursued humpbacks and other whales in every corner of the world's oceans.

Today, although still occasionally killed by a couple of native whaling operations, humpback whales are much more likely to be 'shot' by passengers with cameras on the numerous whale-watching enterprises that have sprung up all over the world. Freed from the perils of commercial whaling for four decades, humpbacks have made a strong comeback in most areas. People everywhere are awed by the humpback's spectacular acrobatics, charmed by its curiosity, and moved by the beautiful song sung by courting males.

Right about the time that last whale was killed, scientists found that humpback whales could be individually identified from natural markings. This discovery became the key to learning about the biology, movements and behavior of living humpback whales, gleaned slowly through long-term investigations that in some places are now well into their fourth decade of study – and which are still seeing some of the same whales they first photographed back in the 1970s.

This is the story of the humpback whale, and a glimpse, in both words and pictures, into the life of one of the most fascinating and charismatic animals on earth. My words are accompanied by a pictorial essay that represents Colin Baxter's experiences photographing humpback whales in many locations across our blue planet. We hope you will find within these pages some of the excitement and fascination that Colin and I share for this remarkable creature, the winged leviathan.

Phil Clapham, Seattle

The Humpback Whale

Many years ago, I was part of a research project studying humpback whales in a large, beautiful bay called Samaná, on the northeastern coast of the Dominican Republic in the West Indies. It was, by the standards of my job with the U.S. government today, a simple project. These days, if I go to sea at all, it is usually aboard a large research vessel which has all the modern conveniences, and a permanent crew of around 25 people, in addition to the dozen or so scientists who sail with the ship on a typical expedition. The cost per day to run this sort of ship is quite literally more than our entire budget for a two-month field season in Samaná Bay in the late 1980s.

Back then, I worked for a small non-profit organization, the Center for Coastal Studies in Provincetown, Massachusetts. We studied humpback whales in summer in the Gulf of Maine, and then followed them to their winter breeding grounds in the West Indies. In Samaná, our research was based on a 14-m sailboat, where the six of us who made up the crew did everything: sailed, cooked, cleaned, and conducted the research. Much of the latter was accomplished using an even simpler craft, a 5-m Zodiac inflatable boat powered by a 30 hp outboard engine. The work was often exhausting: we worked long days in tropical sun, and came back to the sailboat to cook an evening meal, and sort through the day's extensive data and photographs. Yet the rewards were many. In addition to the not-awful fate of spending a winter in the Caribbean, there were countless moments with whales of great beauty, of fascination, of excitement… and occasionally of humor.

One morning one of the crew and I took out the Zodiac just after sunrise and headed out into the bay in search of our first whale. It was, unusually, a flat calm morning; the trade winds had ceased to blow for a few blessed hours, and the water surface was like glass in the early morning light. Neither of us was fully awake, having skipped coffee that day in favor of an early start; and the serenity of the morning didn't seem to

A female humpback whale and her calf rest peacefully from the rigours of the ocean, in sheltered waters on a beautifully calm day. Humpbacks will often sleep at the surface, a behavior known as 'logging' because their still bodies can resemble floating logs.

The tall blow or spout of an adult humpback whale can rise into the air up to ten metres. Four or five breaths are common between dives, when the whale's massive tail breaks the surface before descending below.

demand that we should be in any hurry to make the transition to a fully alert state.

We hadn't ventured far into the bay when I saw the first whale, its tall blow shooting like a pillar of mist into the still air. With no wind, it hung there for a long time and slowly dissipated. I alerted my partner, who was driving the boat and, following the direction I was pointing with my arm, swung the small craft 70 degrees to starboard and opened up the engine. The trick with a whale is to get as close as you can to it before it dives, so you have a good idea of where it went down and can position yourself for the next surfacing.

The whale breathed three, four, five times, then we watched as its great tail rose into the air and slipped gracefully below the surface. We mentally marked where it had dived, but it was still quite some distance out. After a couple of minutes running fast across the smooth surface of the sea, we stopped the boat and shut off the engine at a spot which we judged – with, let it be said, not a huge amount of confidence – to be somewhere near where the animal had disappeared. With luck, we would get closer to the whale on the next surfacing, and maybe the third time we'd actually be able to approach it closely enough to work with it. And so, with this in mind, we waited.

In their winter breeding grounds in tropical waters, humpback whales commonly dive for 10 to 20 minutes; sometimes longer, sometimes shorter. Unlike in higher latitudes in summer when the whales feed, short dives are not the rule; so in a place like Samaná Bay, you usually prepare yourself for a long wait. We sat on the

rubber pontoons of the Zodiac, still not fully awake. The sun was becoming warmer now; that, and the continued peace of the morning, served to lull us into a rather dreamlike state. I could almost feel my breathing become deeper, and I stared idly out across the bay, lost in my own thoughts.

Suddenly, no more than 10 meters from the boat, a huge head broke the surface and some 30 tons of whale rose from the depths in a huge breach or leap, the whole body breaking free of the water. In what seemed like slow motion, the animal spun around, its giant flippers like great white wings, the whale as a whole looking for all the world as if it were bound for the blue sky above. Then, as it hit the peak of its breach, it suddenly crashed majestically back into the water, sending up a giant splash like an explosion to shatter the morning calm.

I don't recall if we both screamed as all this happened. Whether the whale's appearance right next to us was just coincidence or the animal's idea of a joke, we'll never know. But afterwards, we were definitely, unequivocally awake.

Whatever, if anything, the creatures that we refer to as humpback whales call themselves, they are known officially to science as *Megaptera novaeangliae*. If one dissects this name, converting it from the Latinized Greek, it translates as 'the winged whale of New England.' The first part of this name refers somewhat whimsically to one of the humpback's most prominent features, and the one which instantly sets it apart from other large whales: its huge pectoral fins, or flippers. These massive appendages are roughly a third of the length of the animal, and in big humpbacks can be more than five meters long. The second part of the name reflects the fact that the first humpback whale to be scientifically described, by a German naturalist called Georg Borowski, was a stranded specimen found on the coast of New England in 1781.

Humpback whales are not the largest of the whales, and in fact several species exceed them in length and/or weight. The largest, of course, is the blue whale, the biggest of which come in at over 30 m and at weights that likely approach 200 tons. Fin whales, right whales, bowhead whales and sei whales all beat the humpback in size; but still, at a maximum length of probably a bit more than 16 m and a weight of more than 40 tons,

A humpback takes to the air in a giant leap, or breach. It is thought that whales breach for a number of different reasons, ranging from communication to play and just excitement.

our subject here remains one of the largest animals that has ever inhabited our planet.

As far as we can tell, these magnificent beasts have been plying the world's oceans for several million years. The fossil record is notoriously incomplete, and tracing the history of any group of animals is at best a rather messy and haphazard exercise. It is akin to putting together a jigsaw puzzle in which many or even most of the pieces are missing, hidden or broken. Paleontologists stumbling upon fossilized bones are often forced to identify species from partial or damaged specimens, requiring many assumptions or guesses about how what they're seeing relates to similar animals in the record. Animals that have been assigned to the genus *Megaptera*, to which the modern humpback whale belongs, first appear in the fossil record in the period known to geologists as the late Miocene, around six million years ago. Whether they were actually humpback whales, or dissimilar ancestors of the species we know today, is not clear, and the paleontological history of this whale – and of just about every other whale, for that matter – is still described in the scientific literature as 'extremely tentative'.

Whatever those early whales were, they represented descendants of a group of animals that had been evolving in the oceans since their ancestors first made the transition from land to water. This group is called the *cetaceans* (from the Greek word *ketos*, whose meaning is akin to 'sea monster'). They include all of the whales, dolphins and porpoises, and encompass a group of more than 80 modern species that include everything from the smallest porpoise (the highly endangered vaquita from Mexico) to the largest blue whale. Cetaceans are believed to have evolved from a group of four-legged terrestrial mammals called condylarths. General belief has it that these animals were carnivores about the size of a modern hyaena, but again the fossil record is maddeningly incomplete.

Whatever they looked like, it seems that these land mammals lived along river estuaries or at the margins

Like all whales, humpbacks have evolved a sleek, hydrodynamic form.

of shallow seas – probably the Tethys Sea, a large prehistoric body of water whose last vestige is the modern Mediterranean. Either to take advantage of better foraging opportunities, or to escape predators on land (or both), the ancestors of cetaceans began to spend increasing amounts of time in the water. As they did so, they gradually evolved certain adaptations which made living there much easier. Over millions of years, they lost their fur and their hind limbs, their forelimbs were modified into paddle-like flippers, and they developed a powerful tail for propulsion. In addition, the overall form became more streamlined, and the nostrils moved from the tip of the snout to the top of the head, a change which made breathing air at the surface easier. They also evolved an extraordinary ability to dive.

Eventually the result was an animal – or rather a series of species – with a completely aquatic lifestyle.

Humpback whales and their ancestors have existed in the world's oceans for several million years.

Indeed, modern cetaceans cannot exist for long on land: freed by buoyancy from the constraints of gravity, their bones are no longer needed to support the animal's weight as do ours, and cetacean bones are (with one or two exceptions) relatively lightweight and porous. Because of this freedom from gravity, cetaceans have also been able to evolve into some of the largest animals that have ever lived, bigger than the largest dinosaurs.

The completion of this transition to the water seems to have occurred sometime around 45 million years ago, which is when we find the first fossils that are truly cetaceans. The zoological Order as a whole is classified into three groups, or sub-orders: the *archaeocetes* ('ancient whales'), a group that in now entirely extinct;

A feeding humpback whale exhausts water from its partly open mouth, revealing some of the baleen filtering mechanism that hangs from its upper jaw.

the *odontocetes*, or toothed whales; and the *mysticetes*, or baleen whales. It is likely that the latter two sub-orders both evolved from the archaeocetes. The toothed whales include all of the dolphins and porpoises, together with the huge sperm whale and an enigmatic, poorly known group of deep-diving species called the beaked whales.

The baleen whales consist of all the species (except for the sperm whale) that we think of as 'great whales', including the humpback. These animals have no teeth; instead, their mouths contain a huge filtration system called baleen, which allows the animal to filter food from the water in large quantities. Although baleen varies considerably in shape and size from one species to another, the basic principle is the same: hundreds of plates hang side by side from both upper jaws, and the inner surface of the two giant racks that these plates collectively make up is covered with a fringe of hair. The whale engulfs a vast quantity of water and food with its cavernous mouth, pushes the water out through the space between the baleen plates, and traps the prey on the fringe before swallowing it whole.

Modern humpback whales possess all of the remarkable adaptations that have evolved in cetaceans over the eons. Among these is an ability to dive for extended periods. An adult humpback remains underwater for

anywhere from a few minutes to (in extreme cases) more than half an hour; dives tend to be shorter on feeding grounds in summer than in winter breeding areas. In summer humpbacks can probably descend to depths of more than 300 m at need, but most foraging dives are more shallow. Their diving abilities are impressive for a mammal that, like us, must breathe air to survive, but humpbacks are far from the champion divers among the cetaceans. That honor falls to the sperm whale (and probably some of the beaked whales), which can not only hold its breath for two hours in extreme cases, but can also descend to lightless depths close to two miles below the surface. Like humpbacks, they do this by collapsing their lungs when they dive, and holding much more oxygen in their muscles than we do. Indeed, sperm whale muscle is so highly oxygenated – 15-20 times more than ours – that the meat of this species is not dark red, but black.

Humpback whales are accomplished divers. They can hold their breath for more than half an hour, and dive to depths of more than 300 meters.

Like all whales, humpbacks are beautifully streamlined and move with consummate grace through the aquatic realm in which they spend their lives. They are not quite as torpedo-like as some other whales, and possess a number of characteristics which set them apart from other species. At one end, the head is covered with strange knobby bumps called tubercles; the function of these protuberances is probably sensory, since each one carries a stiff hair, or vibrissa, which is connected to nerves in the tubercle. Whalers used to whimsically refer to these features as 'stovebolts'.

On top of the head are two nostrils, or blowholes, through which the whale breathes. Whales are much more efficient breathers than we humans, exchanging up to 90 per cent of their lung capacity with each breath. When they exhale, the force of the air rushing out atomizes droplets of water in the blowholes, like a giant spray can, and the hot air condenses to form the well-known 'blow'.

At the other end of the whale is the mighty tail (or 'flukes'), which can exceed 5 m in width in large

individuals. The tail is the whale's primary means of propulsion, but it also acts as a radiator; the flukes contain a network of blood vessels which can shed excess heat when needed, notably in the tropics.

In between the head and the tail are three very distinctive features. First, on the back is the dorsal fin, which like the tail can serve as a radiator. The size and shape of this fin varies hugely among individual humpbacks, from almost absent to high and falcate. The dorsal fin is set upon a sort of platform which often gives the whale a humped appearance, notably when it arches to dive; hence the species' common name.

Second, by the whale's side are the two huge pectoral fins which give the whale its scientific name. Why this species needs such long flippers – in other whales, the pectoral fins

The most distinctive feature of the humpback whale is its giant flippers, or pectoral fins, which can reach five meters in length.

are proportionately much smaller – is not clear. They almost certainly provide the whale with considerable maneuverability, and recent research by a scientist named Frank Fish has indicated that they are hydrodynamically extremely efficient in their design. Furthermore, when the animals are feeding on their typical diet of small fish or krill they will often bring both flippers forward to act (presumably) as a sort of fence that corrals the prey between them. Whatever their function, the flippers end up as *de facto* weapons in fights between males, since their margins usually serve as a substrate for very large barnacles that can inflict nasty injuries upon contact with skin.

Finally, the external surface of a humpback's huge mouth is characterized by a series of long pleats which run longitudinally from the chin down to almost the navel. The humpback shares this particular characteristic with several other whale species which are known collectively as the *rorquals* (from a Norwegian word that has been variously translated as 'tubed', 'pleated' or 'furrowed' whale). The pleats function when the whale feeds: it takes into its mouth a huge volume of water and food, and the pleats expand – think of an accordion – to increase the capacity of the mouth; the pleats contract once more when the whale flushes the water out and swallows its prey.

Beneath a humpback whale's rubbery skin (which is usually about 1 cm thick) is the secret to its ability to go without food for long periods: the blubber. Blubber not only sculpts the

The humpback's pectoral fins have knobbed edges which appear rough-looking. However, studies suggest that the flipper's design is very hydrodynamic, and actually creates 'lift' in the water.

whale's streamlined form and protects the animal from frigid water that would quickly kill us humans, but also acts as a huge energy store. In summer, whales fatten up by feeding for months in high latitudes; in winter, they do not eat at all, and during this time must subsist on fat metabolized from the blubber store. In a plump, well-fed humpback this blubber is 10 cm or more thick; in some other species such as the Arctic-living bowhead whale, it can be 60 cm deep.

After a gestation of almost a year, a humpback whale starts out life at around 4 m in length at birth, and can grow to more than 16 m as an adult. As with all baleen whales, females are on average about a meter or two

Humpback whale calves remain with their mothers for about a year, separating and becoming independent at some point during their second winter.

longer than males, for reasons which are not entirely clear but which may relate to the advantage of size for energy storage when reproducing. Females produce a single calf usually every two or three years, though annual births are not unknown. The great majority of births occur in tropical waters in winter at the warmer end of their annual migration from cold-water feeding grounds to mating and calving areas in low latitudes.

Being mammals, humpback whale calves subsist on their mothers' milk for the first few months of their lives. The mother actually squirts milk into the mouth of her baby, using what is known as a compressor muscle, located in the two mammary glands on the underside of the whale. Whale milk is around seven times higher in fat content than human milk, and calves grow rapidly as a result. By the time they are weaned and ready for a life independent of their mothers at the end of their first year of life, they are usually around 8-10 m in length.

How long a humpback whale lives is somewhat in dispute. Many big whales (such as blue and fin whales) can likely live to a century, and there is evidence that bowhead whales in the Arctic may actually attain ages of 150-200 years. The existing evidence suggests that humpbacks live to at least 50 years, and perhaps a good deal older than that. The oldest identified individuals in some long-term studies were first photographed in the 1970s; and as of 2012 many of these animals are still alive today.

Between birth and death, a humpback whale will make dozens of long annual migrations, swimming thousands of miles. To find out how we know this, and many other things about this animal, let's turn to the study of whales, a noble branch of science known as cetology.

A Five-Meter Fingerprint

It was, as usual, a windy day on Silver Bank. Silver Bank is a remote reef system 50 miles north of the Dominican Republic which represents the largest humpback whale breeding ground in the North Atlantic, and possibly the world. Even though the bank's northeastern edge has a dense barrier reef which provides a buffer against the prevailing trade wind swells, Silver Bank is often a wet and bumpy place to be in a small boat.

The particular small boat in which I found myself was *very* small: a 4-meter Zodiac inflatable which I and my colleague Rich Sears were using to approach and photograph some of the two or three thousand humpback whales that were present on Silver Bank on that February day in 1984, at the peak of the winter breeding season. Rich is a charismatic maniac, a scientist who pioneered studies of blue whales in the Gulf of St Lawrence; I say 'maniac' with affection because he is known for his seeming obliviousness to the bumps and crashes that assault anyone in his boat as he is driving hard through choppy seas. But I was driving that day, pushing the boat over waves as we attempted to keep up with a fast-moving group of eight or nine humpbacks. This was a 'competitive group', a collection of males all pursuing a single female. Male humpbacks fight pretty aggressively for females, with one male defending his central role next to her and others attempting to displace him from this key position. Fights are common, and include charges, body slams and tail thrashes; it's often spectacular to watch as long as your 4-meter boat doesn't inadvertently become part of the action. This is actually difficult to avoid sometimes, because competitive groups often change direction rapidly and unpredictably; more than once I've found myself in the unenviable position of being part of the group dynamic.

In this case, the main challenger to what we term the 'Principal Escort' – the male next to the female – was a moderate-sized humpback which I had only quick looks at in the general mêlée of the competitive group. Suddenly, the female in the middle of it all dove. She was immediately followed by the Principal Escort, and

Water streams off the body of a humpback whale as it dives rapidly. Such dramatic behavior is common among competing males in the breeding season, as they constantly attempt to keep up with a female and fend off challengers.

then by the challenger. His back arched, his huge flukes rose into the air, and suddenly I found myself looking at a very familiar pattern on the underside of the tail. I yelled to Rich over the wind, 'Othello! It's Othello!'

No, not the Shakespearean character. Othello was a male humpback from the Gulf of Maine, a whale that our long-term study there had seen many times since 1979. I had worked in that project since the autumn of 1980, when I showed up on the doorstep of the Center for Coastal Studies in Provincetown, Massachusetts, and announced that I was in town for the winter, could support myself, and was willing to volunteer. Amazingly, they took me in, and shortly afterwards I was working closely with Dr Charles 'Stormy' Mayo, who a couple of years before had begun a small cetacean research program focused on the humpback whales that fed each summer in the productive waters off Cape Cod. These whales were part of a growing population in the Gulf of Maine. Like humpbacks almost everywhere, they undertook a highly predictable annual migration. Humpbacks worldwide overwinter in many such tropical areas, of which Silver Bank is just one. There, they mate, give birth and – amazingly enough – fast for weeks or months before they return to their feeding grounds in the spring.

We knew before 1984 that Gulf of Maine humpbacks migrated to the West Indies each winter. There, they joined hundreds of others from all over the North Atlantic; indeed, they were very much in the minority, scattered widely among whales from Newfoundland, Labrador, Greenland, and even Iceland and Norway. We knew this because in the early 1970s two scientists named Steve Katona and Chuck Jurasz independently made the revolutionary discovery that humpback whales could be individually identified by the pattern of black and white on the underside of their tails. This pattern, which varies from all white to all black, with every variation in between, is unique to each whale – no two humpbacks have exactly the same tail pattern. Photograph that pattern, and you have a record of an individual whale as good as a fingerprint – except that fingerprints aren't five meters across and visible from a couple of hundred meters away.

From working for three years off Cape Cod, I had the tail patterns of many Gulf of Maine humpback whales in my head, but until that February day in 1984 I had never seen one of them in the West Indies. Yet now, 1,500 miles from home on a windy offshore bank in the tropics, there was Othello. It was the first time he had

The underside of a humpback's huge tail reveals the unique pattern of black and white markings that, like a fingerprint, will distinguish this individual from all others in the population. The patterns vary from all white to all black, and are supplemented by various scars and scratches acquired during the whale's life.

been documented at the other end of the migration. To say I was ecstatic is an understatement: it was a wonderful moment, rather like unexpectedly running into an old friend far from home. And it provided one more data point in our emerging picture of humpback whale migratory patterns.

If all the animals in a population look alike, it is very difficult to learn much about them. With many terrestrial animals, scientists can capture them and either tag or mark them in some unique way so that they can be re-identified in the future. If you look out your kitchen window and see squirrels every day, usually you have no idea whether you're watching a single animal that appears repeatedly, or two or more individuals. But if you can tag or mark them (note: I'm not recommending this!) then you can begin to follow their habits: how often they appear, where else in the neighborhood they might range and how their behavior differs from that of other squirrels.

The same principle applies to humpback whales, except that thankfully we don't have to mark them ourselves. This was not always the case, however. In the early days of cetology, when almost all research was conducted in association with, and for, the whaling industry, scientists were unaware that natural variation in markings could be used to identify any whale in a population. Beginning in the 1940s, British scientists began artificially marking humpback and other whales using what was termed a 'Discovery tag' – named for the Discovery Committee, a scientific body. These tags were about 30 cm long, made of stainless steel, and had a unique number etched on the cylindrical shaft. They were fired into a whale's body from a ship using a 12-gauge shotgun. The idea was that at some point in the future – anywhere from the next day to years later – some of these marked whales would be killed by whalers, and the tags recovered during the butchering of the animal. The unique number on the tag could then be traced to learn where the whale had been marked, and from that one would have an idea of how far the whale had moved between what is termed the 'marking' and the 'recovery' (in this case, 'shooting' and 'killing').

Over the years, the whaling industry shot thousands of Discovery tags into whales of various species all over

A group of three Humpbacks in the Sea of Cortez, off Baja California in Mexico. The whale in the middle shows its black tail, which represents one extreme of the range of patterns in humpback whale flukes.

The serrations on the trailing edge of a humpback's fluke are a natural feature, and their unique pattern helps researchers to identify individuals.

the world, and many of these tags were indeed recovered as the industry decimated whale populations. A surprising number were never found, overlooked during the haste with which animals were cut up on the decks of factory ships; a few were discovered weeks later when the 'cooker' (the boiler used for rendering blubber into oil) was cleaned at the end of an expedition. The tags provided interesting information on whale movements, and much was learned about the connections between areas and populations. But Discovery tags, by their nature, could provide detail on no more than two points in a whale's life: the marking and recovery. Where the whale had been in between was anyone's guess. There were also biases associated with the marking, the largest being that some of the Discovery tags probably penetrated vital organs and killed the animal. In this and many other ways, research which depends upon killing the whale is severely limited in the information it can produce.

These days, it is a very different story. By photographing natural markings on living whales, one can accumulate dozens or even thousands of data points on the whale's movements. This is true not only for humpbacks with their tail patterns, but also for other species. As Rich Sears has documented in the Gulf of St Lawrence, blue whales have a unique pattern of mottling across their huge bodies. Individual right whales are distinguishable by the strange bumps called callosities on their heads; the utility of this feature for photo-identification was first noted by Roger Payne, who since 1969 has directed the longest long-term study of any cetacean, the southern right whales off Peninsula Valdes in Argentina. Gray whales can be identified by the mottling and scars on their bodies, and fin whales by the subtle swirls of marks known as the 'blaze and chevron' on their heads. Since sei whales are frequently the target of attacks by a fish called the cookie-cutter shark, they can be individually identified by the pattern of these circular scars on their bodies, in combination with the shape of their dorsal fins. The same principle applies to many other cetaceans: the best-known example is that of killer whales, which for decades have been identified by the shape and size of their huge dorsal fins, together with the swirling pattern of marks beneath that fin, and prominent scars.

The photo-identification method created a revolution in whale research, allowing scientists to conduct long-term studies of living whales, rather than relying on carcasses supplied by the whaling industry. By simply using variations in natural markings, researchers all over the world have studied many populations of whales and have learned a tremendous amount about their habits. We have also learned that whales are very much individuals, with their own distinctive personalities, habits and quirks of behavior.

But why do we care about these things? Why study whales at all? True, they are fascinating animals, and fun to work with –

As with all cetaceans, research on humpback whales is fraught with the difficulty of studying an animal that spends most of its daily life underwater, largely out of reach from human observers.

but that is not enough to justify all of the funding that has gone into whale research over the past few decades.

The basic reason behind this research is that humans have created major problems for whale populations, and now we need to 'manage' those populations to help them recover. The concept of humans 'managing' a wild species in the world's oceans is a difficult one. In principle, humpback whales should simply be able to exist in a sustainable environment without any necessity of human intervention. Whales did exactly this for many millenia before humans became a problem. I would note that the whaling industry would turn this idea of conservation on its head and say that whales should be helped to recover so that we can hunt them again, or that whales need to be 'managed' – which is usually a whaling industry euphemism for 'culled' – because they allegedly compete with human fisheries.

To 'manage' any species, you need to know some basic, and not-so-basic, things about it. How many whales are there in the population? Is the population increasing or declining? What is the 'population' – what are its boundaries, and how much mixing is there between different populations? Which habitats are most important for the species for feeding, mating and giving birth? Does the population suffer from inbreeding? What are the threats that may be inhibiting recovery? And how exactly should 'recovery' be defined?

One of the key elements in conservation is a knowledge of population structure. Specifically, in order to properly conserve any whale species, one needs to know how many populations exist, and their size and relationship to one another. The importance of this can be illustrated with a simple example. Imagine that there are a thousand humpback whales in a single population – that these animals mix freely with each other, and that they all breed together. Now imagine that each year a certain number of these whales are killed by 'unnatural' causes – whaling, entanglement in fishing gear, ship strikes, et cetera. The impact of these mortalities on a single stock of a thousand whales will be far less than if the thousand animals actually make up two separate populations, with one being 900 and the other only 100 animals. The impact of any number of deaths on a population of a hundred will obviously be a lot greater than if that same number of mortalities is taken from a single, mixed stock of a thousand animals. In other words, you need to know how many populations you're dealing with before you can make sensible decisions about how to help conserve them.

For the purpose of conservation, scientists usually define populations by drawing lines on a map; this is inevitable and convenient, but of course the whales themselves don't recognize such neat boundaries. Here's an example. Currently, scientists at the International Whaling Commission (IWC) recognize seven Southern Hemisphere populations of humpback whales. Each of these populations feeds in a particular portion of the Antarctic, and these feeding areas are linked to specific breeding grounds in tropical waters. For example, humpbacks that feed in what is known as 'Area V' – broadly, the area of the Southern Ocean south of Australia and New Zealand – are thought to breed off the eastern coast of Australia and in western Oceania.

A mother and her young calf cruise through clear tropical waters. Calves remain close to their mothers for almost a year, growing rapidly on a diet of milk that is more than seven times richer in fat than human's or cow's milk.

'Management' of these animals – an activity which could cover everything from conservation measures to setting future whaling catch quotas – is all based on the assumption that this population is largely separate from others (which in turn are managed according to our knowledge of their particular size and structure).

How do we study population structure? There are various methods, most of which involve somehow tracking whales from one place to another, and in the process testing whether our notions of the structure and boundaries of their populations are accurate. For example, if a whale from eastern Australia suddenly showed up in the Antarctic south of Africa, this would challenge the current idea that the Australian population is linked only to feeding grounds in the polar waters south of that continent. How serious a challenge this would represent would depend upon whether such movements turned out to be fairly common, or looked instead like a one-shot case of an 'aberrant' wandering whale. To date, incidentally, no such movement has been detected, although Christina Pomilla and her colleagues did recently record a humpback whale going from the east coast of Africa to the west, switching between the Indian and South Atlantic Oceans. Peter Stevick and his colleagues recently documented an even more dramatic example involving a whale that was first seen off Brazil and later showed up in Madagascar, 5,300 nautical miles away. Were these whales lost, or is such movement more common than we think? We don't know, but the answer may be important to management.

The principal means of tracking whales from place to place are threefold: photo-identification, genetics and satellite-monitored radio tags.

Photo-identification uses the unique markings on the underside of a humpback whale's tail (or different features for other species). As I noted above, this has been used to identify many thousands of individual humpback whales all over the world. Photo-ID has allowed scientists to follow individual whales over periods of literally decades in some areas, and also to document the reproductive success of females and their offspring over several generations.

The second method is similar but more high-tech. By taking a tiny sample of skin from a humpback whale through a biopsy – a dart is fired at a whale from a crossbow, and harmlessly takes a small sample before

Lying upside down at the surface, a humpback whale slams its tail down on the water in a behavior known as lobtailing. The bumpy region on the right is the whale's genital area, which shows subtle differences between males and females.

bouncing off into the water – scientists can examine the whale's DNA and conduct many sophisticated and highly informative analyses. These include determining the animal's sex (which usually cannot be done visually), as well as assessing its maternal lineage, and constructing a genetic profile that allows the whale to be individually identified. As with photo-ID, a humpback biopsy-sampled in two different places can, through genotyping, be unequivocally identified as the same individual. All of these tests and many more can be conducted with a single tiny piece of skin – rather different from the 'whole-animal' sampling employed by whalers.

With either of these methods, an individual whale can be resighted or resampled again and again, giving us ever-more information about its movements over the course of years or even its entire life (something which, needless to say, is not possible when a whale is killed – you get one data point, and that's that). Using these methods, thousands of whales have been documented traveling over sometimes huge distances. For example, in the North Atlantic, some humpback whales have been followed for almost 40 years, and observed at migratory endpoints as far apart as Norway and the Caribbean.

Between these two methods, photo-identification and genetics, we have learned a huge amount about humpback whales. However, what photo-ID and genetics cannot do is tell us the daily movements of animals, or to track their wanderings through the innumerable large areas of ocean in which human observers aren't present. In the South Pacific, researchers may photograph a whale in the Cook Islands or off New Caledonia, and then see it again off Tonga (in fact, many such matches have been made with both photographs and genetics); however, we don't know the many details of where the whale goes in between these brief snapshots of its life. This is where the third technique comes in. By attaching a transmitter to a whale, its movements can be

Calves cannot dive for as long as adults, and must return to the surface more frequently to breathe.

remotely followed on a daily basis by a satellite. The transmitter sends a signal to an Argos satellite, which in turn transmits the data to a ground station – and a scientist with a laptop can access this information from the comfort of an easy chair anywhere in the world. Photo-ID and genetic sampling requires scientists to be next to the animal, and it is impossible to follow the whale in rough weather, or at night, or far from the relative safety of coastal waters. In contrast, a tagged whale can be followed anywhere on Earth, at any time. Not only do scientists get to see the end points, but they learn every detail of the whale's movements without ever having to relocate the animal in the vastness of its huge migratory range (traditional methods require you to find the whale to photograph or biopsy it – and that is as much a matter of luck as anything else).

In New Caledonia, a tropical breeding ground, Claire Garrigue studies the humpback whales that migrate

The shape, size and markings of a humpback whale's dorsal fin vary widely. These features, together with the tail pattern, are used by scientists to identify individuals. Dorsal fins vary from almost absent to high and hooked.

A humpback with an all-white tail begins a dive. The average amount of white or black on tails varies considerably between populations; whales from some parts of the Southern Hemisphere are on average much whiter than those from other areas.

there each winter from the Antarctic. Claire may photograph a whale in the large lagoon off southern New Caledonia where she works; and a few weeks or years later that same whale may be seen almost 2,160 nautical miles away off Rarotonga in the Cook Islands by Nan Hauser, who has worked with humpbacks there since 1998. These matches are very important scientifically; but the whale's movements in between these two far-flung points in time and space are largely unknown. Do New Caledonia whales travel to New Zealand? Do whales in the Cook Islands travel east or west when they leave, or are their movements all over the map? Satellite tagging can address exactly these kinds of questions, and in doing so can provide critical information about population structure and behavior for use in management.

Consequently, in August and September of 2007, we set out to study movement. This wasn't our first venture into tagging in this region: the previous year, Nan's project had placed a single satellite tag on a whale – a mother observed off the main island of Rarotonga – who was watched over four months as the animal migrated from the Cook Islands into the Southern Ocean. By the time the tag ceased transmitting in late January 2007, the whale had traveled almost 2,500 miles to the Antarctic Circle.

The next year, Claire Garrigue and Nan Hauser, working with Brazilian scientists Alex Zerbini and Ygor Geyer, with funding from Greenpeace, succeeded in deploying 19 satellite tags on humpbacks – 12 in New Caledonia and a further seven in the Cooks. All of the scientists working on humpbacks in the South Pacific eagerly awaited the streams of data that came from the tags, and they were not disappointed. Although all the tags ceased transmission before any of the whales reached the Antarctic, the information they yielded was spectacular.

The blow of a whale is its visible breath. It is created partly by condensation of the warm breath in cooler outside air, and also by the atomization of water droplets in the whale's nostrils, or blowholes.

Because by necessity we usually work close to our own coasts, we tend to fall into the trap of seeing humpback whales as coastal animals, yet they are not. Of the 12 New Caledonia tags, several traveled from the southern coastal lagoon to Antigonia Reef, a remote offshore seamount to the southeast, and some of the whales remained there for an extended period. Until then, no one had any idea of the apparent importance of this offshore habitat to the animals.

One whale surprised everyone by leaving the southern lagoon and moving up the entire length of the western coast of New Caledonia, and then traveling hundreds of miles west to the area of reefs and islands known as the Chesterfields. This provided an interesting historical insight, because in Herman Melville's day the Chesterfields had been one site of American 'Yankee' whaling in the 19th century.

Then there were the long-distance migrants. Some of the whales tagged off New Caledonia moved to Norfolk Island and/or to the northern coast of New Zealand, thus filling a key gap in our knowledge of their population structure. We had always wondered where New Zealand whales went (there were only a few photo-ID matches prior to this project). The movements between these two areas are important, because whales in neither area have shown signs of recovery from whaling, and thus the link is a logical one that has significant implications for conservation. In this regard, the fact that none of the whales tagged in New Caledonia moved to Australia provides further support for the idea that the former is a largely separate population whose recovery is not being accelerated by any influx of animals from the much larger Australian population.

In the Cook Islands, the behavior of the seven tagged whales was characterized by one huge surprise: rather than spreading out and traveling in different directions, they *all* moved west. One animal traveled all the way to American Samoa, while others moved through the many islands and reef systems that make up the Tonga group. Does this indicate that whales enter the Cooks in a kind of 'wave' that sweeps through the islands from the east? We don't yet know, although such movement patterns have been observed among humpbacks tracked by photo-ID in another breeding area, the West Indies.

Another surprise was that – even though some tags from 2007 continued transmitting well into October, which is quite late in the season – none of the Cooks whales showed any signs of turning south towards the Antarctic. This is in contrast to the New Caledonia whales, some of whom began moving south shortly after being tagged. The variability in these movements, and the consistency with which the Cook Islands animals all traveled west, have important implications for a variety of issues ranging from population structure to how these animals navigate.

Other scientists have also tracked humpback whales by satellite. Some of the whales in these projects have confirmed knowledge derived from photo-identification studies of the connections between feeding and breeding areas, while others have thrown us for a loop. Several humpbacks tagged in Hawaii by a scientist

Although humpbacks breach in any weather, for some unknown reason they often begin breaching when the wind and sea state picks up.

named Bruce Mate went to Southeast Alaska, just as scores of photo-identification matches between these two places said that they were 'supposed' to. However, one humpback traveled instead along the Aleutian Island chain and ended up at the southern tip of Kamchatka in Russia, a completely unknown destination for Hawaiian whales at the time. The problem was that no one had ever worked on humpback whales in Kamchatka. The study emphasized the sobering point that if you work in just a few areas, you'll get information about only those areas, and will entirely miss the movements of animals that decide to go elsewhere.

It was exactly this problem – of restricted geographic coverage limiting knowledge for management – that lay behind an ambitious project I and my colleagues initiated in the North Atlantic in the early 1990s. Up until then, researchers had studied humpbacks in a variety of places using different methods and platforms, and with very different amounts of effort. This disparity made it difficult to figure out the abundance and population structure of North Atlantic humpbacks, and large areas of potential humpback habitat had never been studied at all.

Rather than continue to collect modest amounts of information over many years, in a non-standardized way, we decided to try throwing everything we had at a big, co-ordinated project that would run for two years. The idea was to have everyone co-operate and use the same methods in a giant study that would cover much of the known range of the species, from the West Indies breeding grounds to feeding areas all the way up to the Arctic. Thus was the 'Years of the North Atlantic Humpback' (YONAH) project born.

There's a simple reason that scientists often undertake small-scale projects rather than big ones: studying whales is difficult, and such work doesn't come cheap. With YONAH, however, we decided to abandon the usual model of 'do what you've been able to afford to do before' and instead design a study that would give us the best data (and thus the best answers) – and then try to raise the money to do it right.

Amazingly, it worked. Researchers from seven countries worked together to craft a unified approach to the study of North Atlantic humpback whales, somehow it was all funded, and the result was a tremendously successful project that yielded a huge amount of data. YONAH combined photo-identification and genetic

Three humpbacks begin a deep dive in Frederick Sound, Southeast Alaska, where whales come each summer to feed. With the exception of mothers with calves, humpbacks do not usually remain with the same associates for long. Instead they constantly change companions, although there are a few examples of long-term associations among individuals in Alaskan waters.

The bumpy tubercles on a humpback's head were whimsically called 'stove bolts' by whalers.

sampling of whales from the West Indies, the Gulf of Maine, the Gulf of St Lawrence, Newfoundland, Labrador, Greenland, Iceland and Norway. In two winters and two summers of field work, we identified more than 3,000 individuals from tail fluke photographs, and biopsy sampled another 2,600 for genetic analysis. There were hundreds of photographic and genetic matches, with the same individual whales being seen in locations that were sometimes thousands of miles apart.

Many scientific papers came out of the YONAH project, including an estimate of abundance for North Atlantic humpbacks, as well as detailed knowledge of the structure and genetic makeup of the population. Among other things, the study confirmed the strong fidelity to feeding grounds among individual whales; whales return to the same feeding grounds year after year, and rarely switch to other areas. Thus, a Gulf of Maine whale will remain a Gulf of Maine whale, and won't suddenly show up feeding off Greenland (and vice versa). Fidelity to specific feeding grounds is a key element of the humpback whale's lifestyle and behavior.

The successful YONAH approach was adopted by humpback researchers working in the North Pacific, in an even larger study called SPLASH (Structure of Populations Levels of Abundance and Status of Humpback whales). Working across the entire North Pacific from North America to Russia and Japan, SPLASH brought together more than 50 research groups and 400 scientists from 10 nations. Working over three winters and two summers in the period 2004-2006, the project collected photographs of almost 8,000 individual humpbacks, and also obtained more than 6,000 biopsy samples – an extraordinary achievement. Known migratory connections were reinforced, and many new ones were established. Overall, the SPLASH project (analysis for which was still underway at the time of writing) will give a thorough picture of the abundance, structure and status of humpback whales in this ocean basin. Like YONAH in the North

Atlantic, the knowledge gained from this remarkable study will form the basis for future management and conservation of humpback whales across the North Pacific.

So, as a result of the various methods and projects described above, these days we know an awful lot about many humpback whale populations. I'll summarize much of this knowledge in the next chapters, but for now I'd like to give you a look at some of the individual whales whose lives and habits collectively make up that story. Any census of a human population hides a rich tapestry of life stories beneath faceless columns of figures, and it is no different with whales. Beyond the numbers, modern whale biology is, at its root, a study of individuals.

Humpback whale's pectoral fins can have different amounts of black and white coloring on the upper (dorsal) surface. Both North and South Pacific whales tend to have mostly black flippers, whilst those in the North Atlantic are more frequently white.

Salt, Silver, Patches, Mars. Streamer, Colt, Midnight, Othello. Sockeye, Comet, Bandit, Flag. We have no idea what, if anything, whales call themselves, but in the Gulf of Maine – where a population of humpback whales has been studied for almost 40 years – we give them an endless variety of names. The names are more than just affectionate appellations: they are based upon markings of some kind on the whale's tail or body. The general idea is that when you see that mark in the field, it will remind you of the name and thus help you to identify the whale. The theory works a lot better on some animals than on others.

Some whales possess spectacular marks that make the individual instantly recognizable. A large female in the Gulf of Maine has an all-black tail with a bright white marking on the left side that looks just like the paw print of a cat, so she has been known for years as *Cat's Paw*. Another female named *Salt* – the first whale ever to be named in this area, way back in 1975 – has a large white scar on her dorsal fin that looks like someone sprinkled a liberal dose of salt on it. A young whale first seen in the late 1980s had a big splat-like pattern in the middle of the left side of its tail; since this mark looked exactly like a road-killed animal, the whale was duly called (over the protests of some), *Roadkill*. Many of us hoped *Roadkill* would never be seen again; inevitably, however, he became resident in the area for several months the following year. As a result, all the local whale-watching tour guides suffered daily embarrassment when they were forced to explain to hordes of tourists why this poor animal had been so uncharitably christened ('And here is our whale called... well, er... *Roadkill...*')

Other whales are less well marked, and we search for obscure scars or other features that might resemble something worthy of a name. All-black tails yield a variety of dark names: *Ebony, Coal, Midnight, Onyx* (et cetera). Similarly with all-white flukes: *Ivory, Snowy, Blanco, Blizzard*. In all, more than 1,500 humpback whales have been identified by natural markings in the Gulf of Maine, and every one of them has a name. As a result, it becomes harder and harder to come up with relevant, unused names.

Every year in the spring there is a Whale Naming Party, to which numerous friends and colleagues are invited. Photographs of the new whales are laid out on tables, and guests are invited to examine them for marks, then suggest names accordingly (after they have checked the existing list, often to find out that no,

The basic pattern on the underside of a humpback's tail is determined genetically, and will remain unchanged throughout the whale's life. This whale shows a number of scars picked up along the way; in particular, the white scuffing on both sides of the tail's base indicate that the animal was at some point probably entangled in fishing gear, a common problem for large whales.

A spectacular leap for the sky. Humpbacks can breach just once, or repeatedly, in some cases more than a hundred times in a row.

that name has already been taken). After everyone is done exercising their imagination, a photo of each whale's tail is projected onto a screen, the suggested names are read out, and after some debate (which usually includes cheers, cat calls and the occasional sarcastic comment), somehow a name is agreed upon.

In the old days, we used to toast each new whale's name with champagne. This tradition was all well and good when we had only 20 or 30 new whales to deal with; but as the number of new whales (and thereby toasts) grew each year, things got rather out of hand. Indeed, the fact that alcohol is served at these events may explain the rather obscure or nutty nature of some names. Fortunately, the whales themselves are oblivious to these embarrassing monikers.

Whales, like people, are very much individuals. Humans often see animals as all doing the same thing, following rules of biology and behavior like automatons, without the complexity of individual variation that makes every human being unique. But ask just about any biologist studying a population of animals, and he or she will tell you that this is not the case. Whether it's lions, tigers or bears – or humpback whales – there is endless variation in personality and behavior.

Salt, the Gulf of Maine female, was first seen in 1975 and has been observed every year since. She has been photographed over two thousand times, in locations as far apart as Cape Cod, Nova Scotia and the Dominican Republic. Salt has had, to date, 12 calves that we know of; and of those, two of her female calves have grown up to produce nine of their own offspring. There are currently three generations in the Salt lineage: today, she is the grandmother of at least nine whales, although whether she is aware of this distinction we really don't know.

As a mother, Salt has always been very tolerant of the many humans who visit her in whale-watching boats each year. Her first calf, a male named Crystal who was born in 1980, was very curious about boats. Salt let him indulge this curiosity with one particular whale-watching vessel off Cape Cod, and eventually she seemed to trust the boat enough to leave her son alone with them while she went elsewhere to feed (the crew often joked that they were running a babysitting service for Salt). That was her first time as a mother; but every time she returns to the Gulf of Maine with a calf in tow, she brings her new baby over to the boat – is this really an introduction?

Some other mothers are not nearly as friendly. A large female named Fringe, for whatever reason, has never seemed to like boats, and issues a sharp reprimand if one of her calves tries to wander over to a nearby vessel (the reprimand is a behavior called a tail breach, where the whale throws her back end sideways out of the water with a very dramatic splash; it's a move guaranteed to have her calf scurrying back to her side).

Many humpbacks are friendly and curious, some absurdly so. A male named Colt who was born in 1981 will sometimes break off from feeding to approach a boat, and will happily swim back and forth underneath the hull for an hour or more, to the delight of the people on board. Another, younger, male named Bandit has a similar fascination with boats, and in the early 1990s everyone in the Cape Cod whale-watching industry waited with some trepidation for the inevitable day when Colt and Bandit would team up. Finally they did, and the result was a boat that was so hemmed in by the two ridiculously curious whales that it couldn't move,

Because humpback whales are individually identifiable through natural markings, scientists have been able to document the return of particular whales to the same feeding ground for periods of more than 40 years.

A young whale shows the sharp line of its jaw as well as the pleats of its mouth which are characteristics of the humpback and several related whale species. This group of whales are termed 'rorquals' from the Danish word for 'pleated' or 'tubed' whale.

and found itself seriously delayed in its schedule. Finally, the captain begged another whale-watching boat to come over and lure the whales away. The boat that heeded the call went bow to bow with the trapped ship and had all its passengers jump up and down to make noise; the whales moved, the first boat escaped, and then the second found itself similarly entrapped. The Colt and Bandit Show had lived up to expectations.

Humpback whales show their individual differences in many ways, from the techniques they use to catch prey to the habitats they prefer, from their tendencies to engage in acrobatic behavior to their preferences for particular associates. Some whales have appealing behavioral eccentricities: a whale named Streamer used to like to play with seaweed, wood, or anything else floating around at the surface, nosing it around on her head (that was when she was young; she's long since become a mother, and is much too old and mature for such frivolity these days). Another Gulf of Maine female, Talon, once engaged in a crude version of volleyball, repeatedly pushing a large round plastic float back to a research vessel after the crew had thrown the float in for her amusement.

Humpbacks also vary quite a lot in their reproductive success. We know very little about how successful males are in this regard, although we have reason to suspect that some males do much better than others in the

mating game. But female reproduction is rather easier to measure, simply because the end product is a very visible calf.

Long-term studies of humpback whale populations have been the key to what we now know. Some of these studies (such as that in the Gulf of Maine and some others in Alaska) are currently in or approaching their fifth decade of continuous research – effectively the length of a professional career for the average scientist. Through the painstaking documentation of tens of thousands of sightings of identified individuals over many years, photograph by photograph, such studies have given us a good picture of the life history and reproduction of this species.

By observing multiple generations of whales – like Salt with her two generations of descendants – we can assess the age at which female whales reach sexual maturity. As it turns out, this varies by area. In the Gulf of Maine in the 1980s, females began reproducing relatively young, at the age of five or six years; the average has since risen to seven or eight. In Southeast Alaska, the average age at which a female gives birth for the first time is closer to 10. These variations among humpback populations probably reflect variable environmental conditions, or differences in the recovery status of the populations. As populations recover from whaling or other sources of depletion, they grow towards what is called 'carrying capacity' – broadly, the ability of the environment to provide enough food resources to support all the animals that depend upon it. If there is a lot of competition for the same food, animals will often be nutritionally stressed, and this can result in their maturing later or reproducing less. By contrast, a small population may have plenty of food, allowing animals to grow fast and reproduce earlier. The situation is of course more complex than this because whales are never the only predators in an environment; but all other things being equal, the principle holds true, and it probably at least partly explains the differences we observe between

A calf no more than a few days old swims close to its mother.

humpback populations in the Gulf of Maine and Southeast Alaska (or elsewhere).

Once they have reached sexual maturity, most female humpback whales produce calves at regular intervals of two or three years (occasionally even one year). Salt is a good example of this – the 12 calves she has had since 1980 have almost all been born on this predictable schedule. Other females seem to be less productive, and appear with calves less frequently. Whether these females conceive less often, or lose their calves before we can observe them, we don't know. Thanks to a study in the North Pacific by Christine Gabriele and her colleagues, we know that many calves die before they ever reach the feeding grounds. They looked at mothers photo-identified with calves in the Hawaiian breeding grounds and matched those observations to photographs taken a few months later in the Alaskan summering areas to see how many of the females showed up with or without their offspring. The results suggested that about one in five calves die before they reach the feeding grounds. Whether these animals are the victims of predation by sharks or killer whales, or are simply too weak to survive their first few weeks of life, we don't know.

Today, we've come a long way since the days when killing a whale was the only way of studying these animals. The modern cetologist can utilize a wide array of methods beyond the ones I've described. A single small skin biopsy can be used not only for genetic analysis, but also to study diet, contaminant burdens, hormone levels, reproductive state and stress, among other things. A whale's length can be measured using photographs or video, and its underwater behavior studied with a tag that records its every movement in three dimensions. Oceanographic sampling – either at sea or remotely from satellites – can characterize the whale's environment and tell us which habitats are the most important as feeding or breeding grounds.

Increasingly, this sort of technology allows us to penetrate the many mysteries that still surround whales and, we hope, to better understand how to help them recover from the devastation that was wrought by commercial whaling. But ultimately much of our knowledge of humpback whale populations today comes down to information that's gathered about identified individuals: painstakingly, year by year, whale by whale.

A young humpback whale breaches close to a reef amongst the islands of Vava'u, Tonga. Whales come to the breeding grounds at Tonga and other areas of Oceania, and feed in the cold waters of the Antarctic far to the south.

The Wandering Whale

Few animals are distributed as widely over the surface of our planet as the humpback whale. You can see humpbacks from the Arctic to the Antarctic and most places in between. They are found in all the major oceans and most of the minor seas. You can find them off the coast, sometimes quite literally a stone's throw from a beach, but you can also encounter them hundreds or thousands of miles from land crossing abyssal depths. They have proven to be a highly successful species that was once abundant throughout the world's oceans; even now, they are making a strong comeback despite almost being wiped out by commercial whaling.

Scientists and whalers have long known that humpbacks undertake a predictable seasonal migration from cold, productive feeding grounds in summer to breeding and calving areas in warm tropical waters. But it is only since the advent of the photo-identification and individual recognition techniques that we have discovered just how extraordinarily long these migrations can be.

On the 28th of August 2001, biologist Kristin Rasmussen and her colleagues were working off the Pacific coast of Costa Rica. Among many other humpback whales they photographed that day was an individual, probably a male, in a group with a mother and calf. The whale was given the reference number CRC1006.

Two and a half years later, on the 10th of December 2003, other scientists photographed a whale far away in the frigid waters of the Antarctic Peninsula. The photos of the whale's tail pattern were duly submitted to the Antarctic Humpback Whale Catalogue, curated at the College of the Atlantic in Maine, where they are freely available to any of the catalogue's many contributors.

A couple of years later, Rasmussen finally got around to running her own photos of the Costa Rica whale through this catalogue. She found that she had a match with the 2001 Antarctic Peninsula sighting.

A humpback whale surfaces among ice within the sheltered waters of the Antarctic Peninsula and its surrounding islands. Whales from this feeding ground make the longest known migration of any humpback, traveling more than 4,500 nautical miles to the waters of Central America to mate and calf.

A humpback whale's long annual migration takes it from productive high-latitude feeding grounds in the summer, to warm tropical waters in the winter.

Astonishingly, CRC1006 had been seen in two locations separated by almost 4,570 nautical miles.

Currently, this represents the longest recorded migration of any mammal (other than jet-setting humans). For years, scientists believed that this record belonged to another cetacean, the gray whale, which migrates annually from breeding areas in Baja California, Mexico, to feed in the remote waters of the Chukchi Sea off Alaska. As it turned out, CRC1006 made the world record by a mere 20 nautical miles, because Rasmussen found that six other humpbacks from Costa Rica had also been seen off the Antarctic Peninsula, at distances from their Costa Rica positions which ranged from 4,480 to 4,550 nautical miles.

As we mentioned earlier, Peter Stevick and colleagues reported the case of a humpback whale photographed off Brazil that was seen again 5,300 nautical miles away in a completely different breeding ground off Madagascar. Whether this represents a purposeful movement, a freak occurrence or a simple navigational error is not known, but it is a movement of a rather different nature than the straightforward breeding to feeding ground migration of Rasmussen's Costa Rican whale.

Humpback whales are indeed among the greatest wanderers on Earth, although their wanderings are purposeful and often predictable in their range and timing. To travel so far each year, and to spend weeks or even months without eating, as they do in winter, must mean that there is a strong advantage to these extensive migrations. Yet remarkably, we do not know what this advantage might be.

The principal reason underlying the migration of most animals is not weather, but food. For example, birds that feed in the Arctic during summer, leave and go south not so much because the weather in winter is bad (although the effect of such harsh conditions on their survival would certainly not be negligible), but rather because there is little that is accessible for them to eat in polar regions at this time. Many mammals that migrate do so to also take advantage of pronounced seasonal differences in the availability of food resources: better here now, better there later.

This is, however, not at all the case with humpbacks and some of the other migratory large whales. Far from traveling to find food, they actually leave it behind and spend the entire winter in tropical regions where the biological productivity is usually relatively low. It isn't that humpback whales wintering in the tropics *choose*

Remarkably, the main reason for the annual migration of many large whale species, including the humpback, is unknown. Unlike many animals and birds, humpbacks do not migrate for food; indeed, they fast for weeks or months while in their tropical breeding grounds.

not to eat: there simply isn't any food for them there. The huge schools of fish and krill that sustain them in high latitudes do not exist in tropical regions.

So why migrate at all? Why fast for weeks or months at a time when you could stay in high-latitude waters and continue to feed? True, the sea is extremely cold in such places during winter, but surely that wouldn't be a problem for an animal the size of a whale, with a full coat of blubber to protect it?

Several theories have been advanced to explain baleen whale migration, and each has its own adherents. Perhaps the most commonly believed is that warm tropical waters confer a major advantage on newborn calves. While calves probably would not die if they were born in the cold waters of the feeding grounds – after all, much smaller animals such as dolphins survive there all winter – it may be that, in warm water, a calf can devote far more of its energy to growth and development, rather than to staying warm. In evolutionary terms, if females giving birth in the tropics had a higher calf survival rate, then more of these calves would grow up and themselves reproduce. That in turn would mean more copies of their genes in future generations, and eventually the population could become dominated by animals with the 'migrant' genes.

This is an attractive idea, but it fails to explain why everyone else in the population needs to migrate. In terms of energy balance, do all whales somehow benefit from wintering in warm water? This is hard to believe given that they are not feeding for the time they're there. Another problem is how the first migrating whales managed to find those tropical breeding areas so far away from their feeding grounds. One version of this theory says that because it is the females that migrate, all of the males follow in order to mate. Again, this is superficially appealing, but given that most female humpbacks reproduce at two to three year intervals, there's no reason why these females should migrate too.

Another theory suggests that humpbacks migrate to get away from high-latitude areas in which killer whales live and hunt. By giving birth somewhere else, they have a much lower risk of losing a newborn calf to predation. However, killer whales are also found in the tropics (although admittedly not in the density they are elsewhere). Furthermore, there have been very few documented attacks by killer whales on humpbacks,

With effortless grace, a whale turns an underwater somersault in clear tropical waters. Although a humpback's thick blubber layer protects it from the harsh temperatures of frigid polar seas, whales must shed heat in their warm winter habitats.

and these predators are rarely or never seen in some well-studied major breeding grounds; given the abundance of newborn calves in such places, one would think that killer whales would flock to such habitats to pick off an easy meal.

A recent theory by John Durban and Robert Pitman suggests that killer whales undertake long movements to tropical waters to help heal and regenerate their skin, which can deteriorate into poorer condition and become beset by parasites in cold waters. Perhaps humpback whales share a need for physiological 'maintenance' too. Or not.

In short, we really don't completely understand why, every year all over the world, humpback whales swim across vast ocean spaces in a round-trip of several thousand miles. And perhaps we never will.

There are many populations of humpback whales in the world's oceans. With one notably odd exception, all of them have a year that is divided into two distinct periods, spatially and behaviorally: summer feeding in high latitudes, winter breeding and calving in the tropics.

The exception is a small population in the Arabian Sea, which – given that the continent of Asia acts as a gigantic barrier to the normal migration north into higher latitudes – stays in this subtropical region year-round. There are seasons of a sort there: in summer, a strong southwesterly monsoon creates major upwellings off the coast of Oman and elsewhere, and as a result the area is unusually productive biologically. Humpbacks in the Arabian Sea have preserved the annual cycle of their species, with both mating and calving taking place in winter. But, blessed with an abundant food source in such warm water, they just don't need to migrate the way every other humpback whale does.

Elsewhere, humpbacks are found feeding in summer over a huge swath of ocean, from middle latitudes to polar waters. Unlike bowhead whales, they are not usually associated with ice, but in some parts of the ocean kept ice-free by warm currents, they can penetrate very far north or south indeed. In the North Atlantic, for example, humpbacks occur to almost 80 degrees North, or just 600 miles from the North Pole. In the Antarctic,

While the exact manner in which humpbacks find their way thousands of miles across open ocean is uncertain, it is clear that they are master navigators. Migrating humpbacks can travel straight-line courses for more than 1,200 miles with better than one degree accuracy.

A humpback whale diving in the waters of Tonga, where they were once the target of a native hunt. In 1978, the King of Tonga issued a ban on the killing of whales, and Tonga is now the focus of an extensive whale-watching industry.

they range down to the ice edge. And in the North Pacific region, they have recently been seen in increasing numbers above 70 degrees, north of the Bering Strait.

Humpback whale winter breeding and calving grounds occur in many places around the world, and almost all of the major ones are around or inside the two tropics (Cancer and Capricorn). Humpbacks seem to like coastal waters or reef systems, perhaps because these habitats tend to be calmer, and may thus offer some protection from wind and waves for newborn calves. Calves are almost all born in winter, after a pregnancy that lasts a little less than a year, and while they are able to independently swim immediately they are relatively small and vulnerable in their first few weeks.

A list of humpback wintering grounds would include many of the exotic coastal areas and island archipelagoes whose photographs adorn travel posters and represent the vacation dreams of working people. In the Pacific, these include (among others) Hawaii, French Polynesia, Fiji, Tonga and the Cook Islands, as well as southern Japan, Mexico and Central America. In the Atlantic, humpbacks breed in the West Indies, the Cape Verde Islands, and off West Africa. Those from the Antarctic head north to various tropical areas, including Brazil, southwestern Africa, Madagascar, both coasts of Australia, and the many island groups of Oceania. And almost certainly to other areas we know nothing of.

Migration connects these far-flung feeding and breeding grounds. Some whales, like those photographed off both Costa Rica and the Antarctic Peninsula, travel more than 4,500 nautical miles one-way on their migrations. Others, such as those in my old study population in the Gulf of Maine, swim a mere 1,300 nautical miles to the West Indies. The exact connections in a particular region seem to depend in large part upon geography, and they differ from ocean to ocean.

For example, in the North Atlantic, humpbacks make up several largely separate sub-populations that feed in different areas including the Gulf of Maine, Newfoundland, Labrador, Greenland, Iceland and Norway; but in winter most of these animals mix in a single common breeding ground in the West Indies. In the North Pacific, there appear to be at least four breeding grounds: whales feeding off California travel to inshore Mexico and Central America, while those summering in Southeast Alaska go primarily to Hawaii. At least some Russian humpbacks migrate to southern Japan and the Philippines, while many of those summering in the western Gulf of Alaska travel to a remote island group off the coast of Mexico. Finally, the whales that feed in the Bering Sea seem to go all over the place, and there is a strong suggestion in the current data that some of these whales migrate to an as-yet undiscovered breeding area somewhere in the tropical North Pacific.

Finally, there are the Antarctic whales. As a general rule, these polar feeding areas in the Southern Hemisphere are connected to breeding areas directly north. Thus, for example, whales feeding in Antarctic waters south of Australia migrate along the coasts of that continent, while humpbacks feeding further west go to the Indian Ocean, and those further east of Australia winter among the islands of Oceania.

There is considerable structure within these migrations, with individual whales returning to specific feeding grounds every year. This phenomenon of 'site fidelity' appears to be maternally directed: that is, you go where

Far from its Hawaiian winter breeding grounds, a humpback whale takes a break from summer-long feeding in the productive waters of Frederick Sound, Southeast Alaska.

your mother took you in your first year of life. If your mother was a Greenland whale, you'll be a Greenland whale; or if she came instead from Norway or the Gulf of Maine, that's where you'll return from tropical waters at the end of each winter migration. Genetic evidence suggests that this fidelity to specific feeding grounds has persisted for millennia – even though it means that many whales end up migrating three times further each year than some others.

One of the enduring mysteries of these migrations is how each humpback whale gets from A to B, when A is separated from B by thousands of miles of open ocean. To put this into perspective, imagine that you are in New York City and you want to 'migrate' for the winter to Florida. It's easy… you know that if you drive your car onto Interstate Highway 95 and go south, you'll end up at your destination, and you won't even need to check your position along the way or know exactly where you are. If there were no roads, and you had to make the trip by boat, it would still be relatively simple: just follow the coast south and eventually you'd get there.

Now let's make it a bit more challenging. You're in Los Angeles and you want to get to New York – and there are no such things as roads. Still not so tough: you go east until you hit the coast, then turn north until you reach New York; this is a rather crude way of doing things, but it would still get you there. But what about if your destination was a small town in the middle of, say, Missouri? With no map and no roads, you'd have a much more difficult time. Going east would get you part of the way, but without constant updates of your position, you'd more than likely overshoot your destination or miss it by hundreds of miles. You could perhaps use prominent landmarks (assuming you knew how their positions related to that of your destination), but still… it would not be easy, especially towards the end of your journey where much more precise navigation was required to find that small town.

Such a feat would be difficult enough, but now imagine being put in a boat in the Caribbean and told to find your way – no, the boat doesn't come with a GPS – to an exact spot off the coast of northern Norway. No landmarks on the way, just five thousand miles of open ocean, with storms and currents deflecting your path.

Migrating humpback whales leave their feeding grounds in late autumn, traveling to mating and calving areas in the tropics. Whales somehow navigate across open ocean to return each year to precise locations on breeding and feeding grounds separated by thousands of miles.

I can't imagine doing this, yet thousands of humpback whales all over the world unerringly make trips like this year after year.

One thing we've learned from placing satellite transmitters on these animals is that humpbacks can travel in amazingly straight lines for long distances. Some of our tagged whales exhibited tracks that ran for more than 1,200 nautical miles with an accuracy of better than 1 degree, despite bad weather and deflecting currents. How they perform this remarkable navigational feat in the (to us) trackless spaces of open ocean is currently a mystery.

Travis Horton from New Zealand is looking in more detail at the tracks of these animals, assessing whether their movements can be linked to discernible features in the ocean, the position of celestial bodies such as sun and moon, or the Earth's magnetic field. There is evidence – some strong, some not so strong – that other creatures such as birds, turtles and fish use one of more of these mechanisms to navigate, and it is likely that some combination of these inborn skills is employed by humpback whales to find their way across the vastness of the open sea.

However they do it, it's clear from the satellite tracks that they know exactly where they are most of the time. Whales don't blunder about the ocean until they hit some large general area near home – they find their way with unfailing precision to exact locations at both ends of the migratory range. For example, individually identified humpback whales from the Gulf of Maine (like Othello, whom I mentioned earlier) have been seen, often repeatedly, on Silver Bank off the Dominican Republic in winter; yet they return each spring to a small patch of water a few miles off the coast of Cape Cod.

Recent research has suggested that humpback whales may navigate using a combination of geomagnetic and celestial cues, but the precise way in which these methods work together remains unclear.

Using satellite tags, we watch as other whales head slowly but surely across the entire North Atlantic, leaving behind the warmth of the Caribbean where they have fasted for weeks. In doing so, they traverse 4,400 nautical miles of open ocean to Norway, crossing the Mid-Atlantic Ridge and making their way, day by day, ever further northeast, no matter what the weather or anything else throws at them along the way, until finally they arrive home. And there, they begin the great banquet that is the feeding season of summer.

A Summer Banquet in Frigid Seas

Imagine, if you can, being a small fish – say, a herring. You're maybe 25 cm long and you're swimming in a school with thousands of your friends in the dark, chilly waters of Southeast Alaska. Suddenly you sense a presence of some kind lurking beneath the school, and the next thing you know there is a wall of bubbles rising all around you. You and the rest of the school instinctively bunch together more tightly, because over eons of time evolution has taught you that this is a good reaction to most predators. Most predators are other, larger, fish trying to pick off single herring, so by packing yourselves in more tightly with your companions you make it harder for them to do that. It's a good response that has worked well to save you in the past.

But not this time. Suddenly, you feel the pressure of water being driven forward as something huge lunges towards you from below. If you and the other fish have any time to react, you can't go anywhere because you have all become completely hemmed in by a circular wall of bubbles, through which you cannot pass. And the last thing your little herring brain might register before you're eaten is a mouth the size of a huge jacuzzi engulfing not one fish, but the entire school. Sadly, you and all your friends have just become a tasty meal for a humpback whale.

Like some other baleen whales, humpbacks eat a variety of prey. But they are unique in the fact that, as we'll see in a moment, they have developed some ingenious methods for catching their dinner. But first, let's review some basics about humpback whale food and feeding, which is the principal occupation of these whales during their sojourn in high latitudes each summer.

Basic fact number one (a reminder): humpbacks eat for only a portion of the year. In summer, they are found in the cold waters of middle or high latitudes, and they spend a good portion of their days and nights hunting

Water pours from the mouth of a feeding humpback whale off Cape Cod, Massachusetts. Whales engulf huge volumes of water and food, then use their pleats and giant tongues to force the water out, trapping the prey on the inside of their baleen, before swallowing it all.

for prey. In winter, when they migrate to the tropics, they fast for weeks or months, living off substantial reserves of fat built up during the long summer food-fest.

Basic fact number two: being very large animals, and ones whose migratory lifestyle requires them to accumulate such fat reserves, humpbacks need to eat a lot. It isn't so much that, proportionately, the amount they consume is any different from many other animals – we think that whales, like us, eat around 3-4 per cent of their own weight every day – but rather that, in absolute terms, this represents a huge quantity of food. A large adult humpback whale may weigh 40 tons, so during a normal day in the summer feeding season the whale may consume between a ton and a ton and a half of food. Put into human terms, that's the equivalent of eating around 12,000 4-oz hamburgers a day (ketchup not included). And humpbacks are small compared to blue whales, the largest specimens of which may consume 6-8 tons of food every day. It is testament to the remarkable productivity of the ocean that the marine ecosystem can support such ravenous beasts. Indeed, the annual global consumption of fish and other marine life by baleen whales is staggering: it's probably in the hundreds of millions of tons.

Within the group of species known as baleen whales, there is considerable variation in diet: they don't all eat the same thing. Right whales consume tiny copepods, zooplankton that are about the size of a grain of rice. Blue whales almost exclusively eat krill, the small shrimp-like crustaceans (the scientific name is *euphausiids*) that are super-abundant in many parts of the world's oceans. Fin and minke whales have more catholic tastes, eating krill or small schooling fish of several types, depending on what's available.

Humpback whales are similar to fin whales in their eating habits. If krill is plentiful, they will consume vast quantities of it; and, like most baleen whales in the Antarctic, krill is the staple diet for Southern Hemisphere humpbacks. Elsewhere, humpbacks will feed on small fish, including herring, capelin, sand lance and sardines. They will occasionally go after somewhat larger fish such as mackerel; however, this seems to be a comparatively rare diet item, probably because mackerel are just too fast to easily catch.

Exactly how a whale finds its food is not clear. Although the waters of high latitudes are very productive,

Humpback whales have a fairly varied diet, feasting on small schooling fish such as herring, sand lance and capelin, or on large swarms of small shrimp-like crustaceans called krill.

such productivity occurs only in specific locations where physical and biological features interact to create suitable conditions.

Every marine food chain begins with phytoplankton, the microscopic plants that underpin everything else in the ecosystem. In order to grow and reproduce, phytoplankton need two things: sunlight and nutrients. Like all plants, they conduct photosynthesis, converting sunlight into energy. But in order to do this, they must have an adequate supply of nutrients, and this in turn is dependent upon certain environmental conditions. Nutrients sink to the lower depths of the water column, and remain at the bottom, out of reach of the phytoplankton, unless something brings them back up. In certain places in the ocean, currents, bottom topography and other features conspire to create what is known as upwelling. This process is often vital to productivity, because it results in a mixing of the water column, with colder, nutrient-rich bottom water being recycled to the surface, where the nutrients become available to phytoplankton.

Upwelling can be caused by (among other things) currents moving over slopes on the seafloor. The water is pushed towards the surface by what are, in effect, underwater hills. In many places, upwelling is a seasonal phenomenon that can result from changes in water temperature. In summer, the upper layers of water heat up, but sunlight cannot directly warm water below about 10 meters deep, and so what often occurs is the establishment of distinct layers: a colder layer below, and a warmer one above (the boundary between the two is known as the thermocline). This stratification, as it's called, prevents recycling of nutrients from the bottom to the surface. However, in fall and winter, as air temperatures drop, the upper layer begins to lose heat faster than the layer beneath, and eventually it becomes colder than the lower layer. Cold water, being heavier, sinks, and this results in a mixing of the layers, with nutrients being returned to the surface. The process can be accelerated by bottom topography and by storms, but the overall result is that phytoplankton are suddenly no longer nutrient-limited, and they can reproduce in vast quantities (a phenomenon known as a 'bloom').

With abundant phytoplankton in the surface layers, the stage is set for the development of a marine food chain. The phytoplankton are grazed upon by zooplankton, the microscopic animals. These reproduce,

A humpback whale surfaces dramatically after lunging into a school of small fish. The pleats on the whale's underside have expanded, enormously increasing the capacity of its mouth.

and are in turn consumed by larger creatures, including smaller fish and krill (and by the skim-feeding baleen whales, notably right whales and bowheads). The fish themselves become prey for the rorqual whales such as humpbacks.

It is the lack of this mixing in most tropical waters that results in humpback whales fasting for weeks or months at that end of their annual migration. There, the surface water never cools sufficiently to sink, so a permanent thermocline is established, and nutrients are never recycled to the surface. Consequently, the phytoplankton production which drives the whole food chain is always low. There are exceptions to this, of course, such as the notable one in the Arabian Sea, where strong monsoon winds cause mixing of the water column and thereby initiate high productivity, of which the local humpback whale population is the beneficiary.

Returning to the question of how whales find food, it is clear that a hungry humpback must locate a suitably productive area. And these oases are not scattered randomly, nor in many places are they that common. Indeed, you can travel through endless miles of ocean and find little productivity, and therefore no whales.

We could plausibly speculate that whales use a variety of cues together with past experience to locate their prey, switching from one cue or memory to another at different scales. So a whale from the Gulf of Maine population will know the general layout of the place, and will remember the hotspots which have been productive in the past. This doesn't guarantee that they necessarily will be productive right now. The conditions that stimulate productivity change with weather, ecosystem dynamics and other factors,

Whales must use a variety of different cues and clues to find good feeding grounds.

so a great feeding area one year may be relatively barren the next. Whales certainly check out different areas, staying if they're productive and moving on if they're not. Indeed, we know from monitoring the movements of whales to which satellite transmitters have been attached that many animals will periodically leave even a good feeding ground to undertake 'prospecting' excursions, presumably to assess the quality of other habitats.

So, first of all, our hungry whale checks out a particular location in the Gulf of Maine. Let's say it goes to Stellwagen Bank, an underwater hill and often very productive feeding area north of Cape Cod, Massachusetts which is frequently host to large schools of small fish (notably a species called the American sand lance). What then? Stellwagen is a pretty big place, the water is dark, and the fish schools represent tiny dots in a large area of water. Certainly particular parts of the bank represent better hunting grounds than others; for example, the southwestern corner of this underwater hill, and the west side, are frequently productive (in part because the topography there creates an upwelling). Whales presumably learn the geography of the bank, though exactly how they know where they are is currently unclear.

A whale spreads its pectoral fins prior to a dive. Humpbacks do this to brace themselves for the effort required to orient and push their huge bodies downward.

Vision is of limited use underwater, especially in the dark, turbid waters of high latitudes where visibility is often only a few meters. Our humpback may be lucky and hear the feeding calls of other whales – sound travels a long way underwater – and in this case he or she can simply head over in the direction of these vocalizations and join the other animals in their fish-fest. If other whales are not the cue, then we really don't know how an animal zeroes in on a specific portion of the bank. Perhaps they can visually assess the ocean floor topography when they dive, or sense the currents or water column structure that is peculiar to a particular spot. Or perhaps like many animals they can read the local magnetic field like a map and know where they are.

Let's say our whale is on the southwestern corner of Stellwagen Bank. Although it is a much smaller area than the whole bank, it's still a lot of space in which to find a school of fish that may be only 50 meters across. At very close range, whales can see fish, but at distances of more than 10 meters vision can't help them in the murky depths of this area. Perhaps they hear the movements of fish, or perhaps they possess some chemical sense that we don't know about.

Curiously, baleen whales probably still possess a functional sense of smell. Smell as we know it is of no value underwater, and indeed the toothed whales such as dolphins and porpoises have almost certainly lost this sense completely. Toothed whales can locate their prey very effectively using echolocation, and so, over the course of their evolution, they have probably dispensed with a traditional sense of smell; this is reflected in the fact that the olfactory lobe in the brains of toothed whales is greatly reduced in size, and thus probably has little remaining function. This is not the case with baleen whales like humpbacks; as far as we can tell from their anatomy, they possess a good nose (their blowholes) and an olfactory processing unit in their brains that remains large. That baleen whales should have retained a sense of smell isn't surprising: they lack echolocation, and while smell cannot be used under the water, it still has value above, at the surface. If you stand on a boat downwind of a patch of plankton or even sometimes a school of fish, you can easily detect it with your nose (zooplankton patches sometimes smell rather like popcorn). It's quite likely that a downwind whale, inhaling at the surface, can detect either fish schools or the planktonic productivity that marks a good spot to go foraging.

Whatever the case, whales are extremely good at finding food. And humpbacks in particular are also very accomplished at catching it.

We will never know when, in the long course of the species' evolution, a particularly clever humpback whale first figured out that blowing bubbles was a good strategy for catching fish. This fascinating and ingenious behavior, which some scientists consider akin to tool use, may have developed eons ago, or relatively recently.

The use of bubble structures to concentrate fish has been observed in many humpback whale populations,

Lunging on its side, a humpback feeds in the waters of Stellwagen Bank off Cape Cod. The lower jaw is to the left; the rack of baleen that serves as the whale's filtration system can be clearly seen hanging from the upper jaw on the right.

and one of the more interesting aspects of this behavior is that whales from different areas utilize different bubble-feeding techniques.

The most famous of these, often featured in *National Geographic* magazine and on TV nature specials, is the bubble net. Creating a bubble net takes remarkable skill. The net consists of a series of large bubble columns, each a meter or two across; to make an effective bubble net, the whale must swim in a tight spiral beneath a school of fish, releasing bubble columns at precise intervals to form the net, with the whole act timed so that the whale can lunge into the middle of the net just as it closes. The bubbles serve at least two purposes. First, they hem fish in by creating a wall around them. The fish stand little chance: they are trapped by both the bubble wall and by the water surface above (and as anyone who has taken a kayak through white-water rapids knows, you cannot easily paddle – or swim – through air). Second, the bubbles very likely stimulate the most common anti-predator response in the fish, which is to close up the school. This works well against any predator that is trying to pick out a single fish, but it is exactly the wrong reaction to a whale. By bunching up more tightly, the fish merely makes it easier for the whale to engulf the entire school, or at least a large portion of it. Which is, of course, the point. These ingenious nets are the most common bubble structure used by Alaskan humpbacks.

In at least some areas of the North Atlantic, a different bubble structure predominates. Although we do see humpbacks using bubble nets in the Gulf of Maine, the majority of whales instead blow what we call a bubble cloud. This consists of one or more huge bursts of bubbles, probably released from the mouth rather than the blowholes, that form a gigantic cloud rising to the surface. Unlike with a bubble net, there is no free water inside the bubble wall – the cloud engulfs the fish school, making it impossible for them to swim (or see), and traps them against the water surface. But the overall effect is similar: the fish become more concentrated and cannot disperse, allowing the whale to complete the action by lunging with mouth wide open through the cloud, engulfing the fish.

Interestingly, bubble clouds are completely unknown in Alaska; they appear to be a specialization developed

A large group of humpback whales feed together using a bubble net in Frederick Sound, Southeast Alaska. Recent research using tags that record a whale's exact movements has shown that humpbacks construct these 'nets' by blowing precisely timed columns of bubbles to form a circle or spiral around schooling fish, forcing them to pack together and thus make it easier for the whales to engulf them.

If fish or krill schools are considerable, humpbacks will sometimes feed co-operatively in large groups. Here seven whales in the waters of Southeast Alaska crash through the surface together in a spectacular feeding lunge. Whales co-operating to engulf schools of fish often occupy distinct positions and roles within the group.

by North Atlantic humpbacks. What's more, the use of either nets or clouds in the Gulf of Maine population is very specific to individual whales. Most whales use bubble clouds, but a minority employ nets – and it is almost always the same individuals that do this.

Some whales have figured out different techniques, or added refinements of their own. One whale, a male named Sirius, has occasionally been known to herd fish against the side of a boat. The large female named Cat's Paw has a unique and spectacular feeding style that involves blowing a bubble cloud, rising vertically through the surface so that her body is halfway out of the water, sinking down again, and only then lunging through the cloud into the fish. We are not entirely sure what this remarkable behavior achieves, but it seems likely that by rising up and then sinking down vertically, Cat's Paw huge body creates a large whirlpool effect in the bubble cloud that acts to disorient and concentrate the fish even more.

One can often see single humpback whales bubble feeding, but this ingenious behavior becomes even more remarkable – and spectacular – when it is practiced by closely co-ordinated groups. If you're around a big aggregation of humpback whales at a time when they are feeding on fish, then you may be fortunate enough to witness one of the most breathtaking sights in Nature: a group of whales bubble-feeding together.

First the whales dive, one after another or together, their great tails rising majestically into the air. There is a pause during which nothing is seen and nothing happens, and everything appears deceptively calm. Then comes the delicious moment when you suddenly see bubbles rising from the deep, the net or cloud forming at the surface... and I would venture to state that there is not a single whale biologist in the world, no matter how experienced or jaded, whose eyes will at that moment not be riveted to the spot, in breathless anticipation of what is about to happen. For a few second later, mayhem

Five humpbacks are visible here in this feeding group. The two whales in the center show greatly distended pleats which will shortly contract to force water out of the mouth through the baleen.

erupts. The water boils as the humpbacks crash through the surface as a group, their giant mouths wide open as they collectively engulf tons of water and fish. After the initial dramatic lunge, the whales coast at the surface for a few seconds, straining the water through their baleen and swallowing the fish that are trapped in those cavernous mouths. Then they arch their backs and dive to begin the cycle once again.

If the prey are especially abundant, loosely aggregated groups of whales – in extreme events as many as 20 or so – may lunge together into the fish schools. The number of animals that can work together as a group is determined by how big those schools are. In the most interesting cases, groups of closely associated whales work together to herd and capture food. Although many of these groups don't remain together for long periods, there are a few instances where the same individuals have been seen practicing co-operative feeding behavior over many years.

Within such closely knit groups, there appear to be distinct roles in the process of herding fish. Fred Sharpe, who works in Alaska, has documented a group of humpbacks whose bubble-feeding seems to be co-ordinated by means of sound, with one vocalizing individual taking the lead and uttering a series of sounds, culminating in a distinct call to initiate the lunge. It is one of the more remarkable examples of co-operation within the animal kingdom.

Another observation we made in the Gulf of Maine was the rapid spread in the 1980s of an apparently novel technique called kick feeding. Here, a whale would slap the surface of the water with its tail (once or repeatedly), dive, blow a bubble cloud, and then lunge. Whether the kicking behavior stunned fish or acted to somehow concentrate them further isn't clear, but the way in which this new feeding method spread through the population was fascinating.

I distinctly remember being on a whale-watching boat one sunny day in the summer of 1982 and seeing a mature female named Columbia performing this behavior; it was the first time we'd ever seen it. To begin with, we thought the tail slap was random, but as Columbia continued to feed, and continued to execute this maneuver in a precise sequence, it became apparent that the kick was an integral part of her prey capture technique. That year, a small handful of whales were seen kick-feeding. The next year there were more kick-feeders in the population, and – as documented by Mason Weinrich and colleagues – by 1989 fully 50 per cent of the population was using it. It was a dramatic example of cultural transmission, of whales apparently observing others using this technique and then copying it for themselves.

One notable feature of bubble feeding, anywhere it's observed, is that it works on fish but not, apparently, on krill. We don't know whether this is because krill are easier to catch than schooling fish, or whether the bubbles don't stimulate the 'bunching-up' response that occurs in fish. Either way, humpbacks feeding on krill often execute rather more leisurely lunges, often on their sides.

A whale off Cape Cod slams its tail on the surface as it dives. Shortly after, it will lunge through the surface and engulf a large quantity of small fish. This 'lobtail feeding' is a specialization which is practiced only by certain individuals in some populations. In the Gulf of Maine, the behavior spread rapidly after its initial appearance in 1982.

How much is in a mouthful? Like all rorquals, humpbacks feed by lunging into their prey, huge mouths agape, engulfing a vast quantity of water and food. Then the mouth partly closes, water drains out through the giant filter of the baleen, and the fish trapped inside the mouth are swallowed whole. Incidentally, while the mouth of a baleen whale is truly gigantic, the gullet is surprisingly small, and only small fish or krill are targeted as prey.

To date, no one has calculated how much water and food a humpback takes into its cavernous mouth during a lunge, but this has been estimated for a larger species, the fin whale. Jeremy Goldbogen and colleagues recently calculated that a 20-m fin whale can potentially engulf more than 80 cubic meters of water during a lunge. Incredibly, this is actually a larger volume than that of the whale's entire body. The animal achieves this amazing feat by greatly enlarging the capacity of its mouth by expanding the pleats on the underside of its body, a capability also possessed by humpbacks and other rorquals. Fin whales, which are normally the sleekest of all the whales, look like giant tadpoles when they are at the peak of a lunge; then the water is flushed out, the pleats contract, and the whale returns to its normal size and shape.

No matter whether the target is fish or krill, each lunge is driven by the whale's huge tail, and this act is not a trivial undertaking. To appreciate the energy involved in a feeding lunge you need to think about what it would be like to take into the water with you a bag larger than your own body, and then to try to swim as fast as you can while this bag was filled with water. A lunging humpback or fin whale is immediately slowed almost to a stop by the tremendous drag created from the thousands of gallons of water (and prey) rushing into its expanded mouth. That a whale can force its way forward to successfully capture a school of fish or krill is a remarkable testament to the great power of these animals. There are very few sights in nature as thrilling as watching a group of humpback whales crashing through the water surface together in a rapid feeding lunge, huge mouths wide open, and fish flying out of the water ahead of them.

All over the world, humpback whales begin arriving on their various feeding grounds in spring. Whether they

Its giant mouth open and ventral pleats extended, a humpback whale feeds on small fish on Stellwagen Bank off Cape Cod, Massachusetts. The mass of light-colored hairs on the inside of the baleen below the upper jaw act as the filtration mechanism.

A humpback calf rests on its mother's head. Mothers can lose a third of their body weight during the year they are nursing.

are returning to familiar waters off Alaska, Russia, Greenland, Iceland, the Gulf of Maine or (for Southern Hemisphere populations) the Antarctic, they immediately set about the business of restoring their fat reserves.

Newly pregnant females are among the first to arrive from the winter breeding grounds; once they have conceived, there is no reason for them to linger in the tropics, and they must spend as much time as possible packing on weight in preparation for the birth of their calf in the following year. Nursing is a very demanding business for a baleen whale, because the milk that a mother delivers to her calf is very rich in fat. As a result, during the approximately twelve-month period that she is nursing her calf, a mature female humpback will lose perhaps one-third of her body weight; for a big humpback, this can translate into more than 10 tons.

Mothers with calves born that winter are often among the last to leave the breeding grounds and thus often show up later in high latitudes. Some mature males may linger there also, perhaps hoping to pick up a last few matings before the energetic cost becomes too great and they must once again head to the feeding grounds to replenish the fat stores in their diminished blubber layer.

While males frequently compete on the breeding grounds, in feeding areas co-operation among all humpbacks is more the theme. Whales will often feed together, joining forces to hunt and capture prey. For the most part, these associations are short lived; indeed, two whales may feed together for a single lunge, then separate or join other animals. This fluidity seems to be characteristic of baleen whale association patterns generally. There are no 'families', except for the one-year bond between mother and calf, and protracted associations between individuals are quite rare. This stands in sharp contrast to the social behavior of many toothed whales; with killer whales, for example, individuals remain with their family group for their entire lives.

We do see some extended associations between individual humpbacks, and these can last days or even weeks, however, most associations are briefer in nature, and in summer may well be governed in part by the abundance of prey in a particular spot. Large schools of fish or krill will promote foraging by bigger groups of whales, while smaller food patches will be exploited by single animals or pairs. Given that the prey schools vary considerably in size even in one area, this partly explains the changing nature of a humpback's association patterns – group size fluctuates with the size of the prey patch. With very large shoals of fish or krill, groups of more than 20 whales can sometimes be found feeding together.

Humpback calves, like most young mammals, enjoy play and gradually become more independent.

There are some remarkable exceptions to the general rule of transience and fluidity in humpback whale associations. In Southeast Alaska, scientists have documented a group of whales that has generally remained together for years. Individuals come and go with time, but by and large the core members of this group remain associated across an entire summer feeding season and beyond. This is such an extraordinary exception to the general pattern of humpback whale social behavior that it has fascinated researchers. It seems that the animals concerned have learned to feed very effectively as a co-operative unit, working together to herd and capture large schools of herring. Not far away, other humpbacks feed primarily on krill, and no such stability is observed in their associations.

Very little sexual activity is believed to occur in summer, but this behavior isn't entirely absent. Examination of pregnant females killed by the whaling industry revealed fetuses in summer that were too small to have been conceived in the winter. Evidently the occasional mating (and conception) takes place on the feeding grounds, although it's clear that this is not a common event. Male humpbacks also sporadically sing on the feeding grounds; singing is a behavior clearly linked to breeding, and found primarily in the tropics. Nonetheless, levels of testosterone and sperm production in males are much lower in summer than in winter – the physiology of the animal is geared to mating on a largely seasonal reproductive schedule.

All through the long days of summer, humpbacks feed, roaming around between habitats in search of fish and krill. But then summer passes into autumn, and the days become shorter and the air colder. And so, before the icy winter sets in, the whales once again respond to an ages-old call to migrate. We know very little about what cues a humpback whale to one day cease its feeding and head out across sometimes thousands of miles of open ocean towards the warmth of the tropics.

But go they do, fat and ready to breed, leaving behind the frigid waters of high latitudes. They also leave behind – notably where the males are concerned – all thoughts of co-operation. For the next few months, competition – sometimes quite violent in nature – will be the order of the day.

Although only six humpback whales are visible here in Frederick Sound, the telltale blows of four more who have already disappeared beneath the surface still hang in the still Alaskan air.

Winter Romance in the Tropics

For humans, finding a mate involves a wide variety of strategies ranging from witty repartée and gifts to personal ads. However, while fights between men over women are not unknown, they are, thankfully, fairly rare as a consequence of the mating game.

But imagine that you're a man: you see an attractive woman and you go over to try to seduce her. Perhaps she's even interested in you, at least enough so that she doesn't disappear on you. Things seem to be going pretty well. But then suddenly you and your date find yourself surrounded by other men, some of whom start jostling you and trying to push you out of the way so that they can occupy the place at the woman's side. Many of these rivals are big, and all of them have hard, sharp, nasty-looking protuberances on their arms and bodies. Some of them charge you and slam into you with their heads or legs, or body-slam you from the side. They may even butt heads with you. The hard protuberances slice into your skin and cut you, and some of your own anatomy – your nose or ears, or anything that sticks out – becomes bloodied and raw during the mêlée.

The fight may go on for several hours, at the end of which you might still be with the woman, or you may have been displaced by someone larger, meaner or sneakier than yourself. If you *are* still at her side when everyone else finally gives up and goes away, your reward may be a successful seduction. Or it may not.

This, essentially, is a description of what male humpback whales endure innumerable times over the course of the average winter. Humpbacks, while they are often friendly (and never aggressive) towards humans, are far from gentle with each other when it comes to the all-important business of winning a mate.

As we've seen, humpback whales divide their year into two distinct parts. In summer they feed and (mostly) don't mate, while in winter they breed but don't eat. The division of the year is also reflected in hormonal

Male humpbacks eagerly follow a female in a competitive group in the Sea of Cortez, Mexico. Competition is the order of the day among males during winter; a single female can sometimes be pursued by as many as twenty or thirty males, some of whom will fight for the opportunity to mate with her.

Competitive groups such as this one involve males jostling for position behind a central female, and often lead to very aggressive interactions.

changes: females come into estrus in the winter, and testosterone levels in males rise significantly.

Although we probably know more about the humpback whale's mating system than that of any other whale, there remain many mysteries about the love life of these giants. Amazingly, and despite the fact that scientists have spent countless hours and years observing humpbacks on their breeding grounds, they have only very rarely been observed in the act of mating (and to date no one has documented this in the scientific literature). Partly this relates to anatomy. A humpback's penis is fibro-elastic in nature (not vascular as it is in humans), and animals with this kind of reproductive equipment tend to mate fast. Still, it's surprising that the act of copulation itself has never been witnessed, even by those scientists who have spent a great deal of time looking at humpbacks underwater. Incidentally, to avoid obvious problems of drag, the male's penis is internal, but can be extruded during copulation.

One of the other great mysteries about humpbacks is why males sing long, very complex songs that change over time. While much has been learned about what male humpbacks do during the winter breeding season, we still have very little idea of how females choose a mate.

Here's what we do know. First, most mating and calving occurs in winter. We know this because in addition to frequently observing mating-related behaviors at this time (and rarely in summer), examination of innumerable pregnant females killed by whaling has shown the length of fetuses to be consistent with winter conception. Fetuses are very small in winter, increasingly large during summer and fall, and approach an average length of over 4 m at birth. Very occasionally, a fetus was examined that didn't fit this pattern and was clearly the result of a summer mating, but such 'aseasonal' conceptions are clearly not the norm.

Second, males compete often aggressively for females. A male humpback will latch on to an adult female, and will then often be challenged for his prime position next to her by anywhere from one to more than 20 other males. If you are a male humpback whale and someone else is attempting to take what you regard as your woman, you have various options available to you depending on your size, strength and motivation.

In what is probably an attempt to make himself appear larger, a male humpback inflates his ventral pouch in a threat display aimed at other males.

At the most basic level, you will always seek to ensure that you are between the female and the challenging male. You may expand your huge mouth, perhaps in an attempt to look large and intimidating, and you might also release long streams of bubbles as a warning, or to create a temporary screen to confuse your opponent. If that fails to discourage him, the conflict may escalate into direct contact. You might ram the challenger, or slash him with your huge tail or flippers – which have very nasty, sharp barnacles attached to them.

These 'competitive groups', as they are called, can be brief or last for hours. Groups will often pick up or lose members, and only some of the participants will be actively involved in challenges to the lead male (or 'Principal Escort', as he is known). Others hang around on the periphery, either too small or too timid to enter the fray, or perhaps hoping to sneak in while the prime players are distracted by the action.

Big competitive groups represent one of the most exciting spectacles in nature. There is much charging, splashing and thrashing around, with constant changes of direction and sometimes quite violent contact between participants. Watching 40-ton animals fight is undeniably a thrill – unless one is following in a small boat which, through a change in the group's direction, suddenly finds itself in the middle of the battle. This has happened to me a number of times (part of the work for my PhD was figuring out the structure and make-up of competitive groups), and while it does tend to concentrate the mind, I have always been amazed at how careful humpback whales are, even in such a chaotic situation.

At some point, the group will break up, leaving one male the victor, but whether this success in battle guarantees him the female's sexual favors is not known. In keeping with what one would expect, there is some evidence that larger males are more likely to be Principal Escorts. Equally interesting is the discovery by Adam Pack, Louis Herman and colleagues, from work in Hawaii, that males prefer larger females. Many scientists have assumed that male animals will mate with any available female, but we know from research on easier-to-study terrestrial mammals that this isn't always so. It makes sense, especially in a mating system which features high-energy, aggressive competition. After all, while males have nothing to do with pregnancy or the

A male on the major North Atlantic breeding ground of Silver Bank, north of the Dominican Republic, is 'beached' on the back of another whale as the latter moves to block his competitor's access to a female.

subsequent rearing of offspring, they have only a finite amount of energy to expend (remember that they don't eat for the entire winter); consequently, it's not surprising that they should be at least somewhat selective in their choice of mates.

We have absolutely no idea what females think of all of this, nor of what criteria they use to select a male to mate with. By and large, females in competitive groups seem to just go their merry way while pandemonium erupts around them. However, since they bear the great bulk of the reproductive effort, they are presumably even choosier about partners. A typical female will give birth to a single calf on average every two or three years, and we know from genetic paternity analysis that multiple calves born to a particular female are fathered by different males. In other words, there's no mating fidelity between pairs of whales across years. Mate choice in humpback whales is certainly not random – it is very much in a female's interest to pick a male who will contribute good genetic qualities to her offspring – but how females settle on a particular mate is unknown. The size and/or strength of a male are obvious candidates, and a female could assess such characteristics visually, or through the outcome of competitive encounters with other males. Or perhaps another way to judge a male's 'quality' is to assess how long he can hold his breath.

Which brings us to the great melodic mystery of humpback whale behavior: song.

In biology, a song is any series of sounds repeated in a pattern. Songs can be as simple as the two-note chirp of a cricket, or as complex as some of the vocalizations produced by many birds. Humpback whales also sing, and for sheer complexity their songs are hard to beat. A song consists of notes that are repeated to make up a theme, and there are anywhere from two to around ten separate themes within a song.

A male escort keeps watch over a female and her new calf.

Only males sing. Remarkably, all of the males within a given population sing the same song, and that song will be radically different from those sung in other populations; a humpback whale in the West Indies sings a very different tune to one in, say, Hawaii. Even more remarkably, the song changes progressively with time, yet all of the whales somehow keep up with the current version. How they do this is entirely unknown. *Why* they do this – why the song constantly changes – is perhaps the biggest question of all.

There are essentially three camps among whale biologists concerning the function of the song. Most believe that it is primarily to attract females – that it is a display similar to the innumerable male displays of other species. Another group note, from research led by Jim Darling in Hawaii, that when singers are joined by other whales, those animals are invariably males, not females, and they argue that song's primary function is to mediate interactions or spacing among males. The final camp (which includes me) believes that both ideas have merit, and that there isn't just one reason behind why males sing.

And sing they do – for hours or days sometimes. Although most song occurs in winter in the breeding grounds, it is commonly heard on migration routes and sometimes also in feeding areas in summer. If song takes little effort to produce, then it may represent cheap advertising for males, no matter where they are. Song can travel many miles when the whale is in deep water, although the higher-frequency portions of the song are much more limited in their range. Humpbacks can't hold a candle to blue whales, whose low-frequency vocalizations are the loudest in the animal kingdom and which, with the right conditions, can be heard over distances of more than 1,500 miles.

A male humpback whale hangs in the water, head down, in a typical singing pose.

The length of a humpback whale's song varies with the whale singing it, and here is where the song may act as a way of advertising quality, as reflected in the ability of a male to hold his breath for an extended period. Singers tend to surface to breathe at the same point in the song, and while they continue to sing at the surface, the sounds becomes quieter because of a phenomenon called attenuation. This characteristic would potentially allow a female to monitor the length of a male's dive, perhaps giving an indication of his endurance. This idea, which was first put forward by Kevin Chu, is of course speculative. Indeed, it would be very difficult to test, because you would have to gain information on the mating success of many males with songs of differing length – and no one has ever seen humpbacks mate.

Why does the song change? Do females value novelty? Who initiates the changes, and how does the rest of the population keep up? A fascinating hint came some years ago when Mike Noad and colleagues were acoustically monitoring humpback whale song off the eastern coast of Australia. There, humpbacks travel north along the coast as they migrate from Antarctic feeding grounds to breeding areas that are believed to be in the Great Barrier Reef region. At the end of the winter, they pass the coast again, this time heading south. In 1996, two whales (among hundreds monitored) were singing a completely different song from everyone else. As it turned out, the song was that being sung off western Australia, where a different population of humpback whales make the same migration on the opposite side of the continent.

During the northward migration the following year, the 'western' song had become more common. And by the time the whales returned south a few weeks later, almost *all* of them were singing the new song. This was nothing less than a cultural revolution. Evidently there was something in the western song that worked better

Breaching is common in breeding areas, and is often thought to be a sign of excitement. This humpback leaps out of the water off the coast of Baja California, Mexico.

than the old version; but it is not known whether the motivation for so many whales to make the change was somehow seeing increased mating success among males that adopted the new song.

Since then, Noad's PhD student Ellen Garland has used song recordings from scientists in the South Pacific Whale Research Consortium, working in locations ranging from Australia to French Polynesia, to study the spread of the humpback whales' song across the vast aquatic realm of Oceania. Like 'cultural ripples', a particular song spreads eastwards across the Pacific like a wave, taking two or three years to engulf the entire region. The geographic scale of this cultural change appears to be unparalleled in any other species except humans. We have no idea how it's accomplished – or why.

But does humpback whale song really constitute 'culture'? That of course depends upon how one defines the term. Like everything else, we humans tend to define concepts such as intelligence and culture according to our own biased, anthropocentric frame of reference. Contrary to popular romantic notions, there is no evidence that humpback whales have what we would call 'language', which at a minimum involves rules of syntax and grammar, and the abstract communication of concepts through a commonly accepted vocabulary of words.

However, they probably do have culture of a sort. In addition to the fact that song is different among populations, and is transmitted across large areas of ocean, the songs themselves have another feature which represents a possible parallel to the way in which humans sometimes remember and transmit information. In 1988, researchers Linda Guinee and Katy Payne noted the occurrence of what they termed 'rhyme-like repetitions' in the songs of humpback whales. Furthermore, they noted that these repetitions tended to occur, like human rhymes, in 'highly rhythmical contexts' within the song. They suggested that, like us, humpback whales use rhymes as mnemonic devices.

What are male humpback whales 'saying', singing as they do for hours or days, and sometimes in the lonely spaces of a vast ocean? Whatever it is, the chorus of song is, to anyone who has heard it, grand, haunting and unforgettable.

Humpback whale song can travel considerable distances underwater. Although singing is heard at all times of the year, including occasionally on summer feeding grounds, it is a central feature of winter breeding areas.

The Whimsical Whale

Until not so long ago, seeing a humpback whale jump out of the water must have been a quite terrifying experience for anyone in a small boat, especially if the person concerned had never seen a whale before. Indeed, it can be a terrifying experience even if you know humpbacks well. If you had been a fisherman in the ancient or medieval world, the sight of a 40-ton sea monster suddenly leaping into the air and crashing back into the water with a huge splash would likely have been enough to have you rowing for dear life in the opposite direction, no doubt praying fervently to all the saints as you went. Later, you would tell your family the tale of your miraculous escape from the demon of the deep. For such was the view of whales for centuries, as 'monstrous fishes' that many saw as dark emissaries of the devil.

Today, we know better, and breaching, as the behavior is called, is perhaps the most spectacular act one can witness from a humpback, and must rank as one of the most thrilling sights in the animal kingdom. In the classic breach, humpbacks leap head first out of the water, often spinning slowly as they briefly fly. Surprisingly, it doesn't seem to take too much effort to jump… a few strokes of that powerful tail and they're out of the water. Humpbacks aren't the only whales that breach, but they do so more often than any other. A whale may breach once, or more than a hundred times in succession. So why do they do it?

What is clear about breaching is that it serves more than one function, and depends a lot on context. Humpback whale calves breach often, and it's likely just play. Adults also do it, alone or when in a group. It is seen in all weathers, but often occurs quite predictably when the wind speed suddenly increases and the sea surface kicks up. While you can never know exactly what goes through a whale's mind prior to a breach, you can often make a good guess. Sometimes breaching seems to be a way of signaling position to other whales, and sometimes it is clearly excitement.

Spray flies off a humpback whale as it leaps from the water in a huge breach. Despite the strength needed to perform this action, breaching is accomplished with surprising ease; a whale can jump out of the water after just a few strokes of its powerful tail.

Disturb a whale and sometimes it will breach. I once sneaked up on a whale that was sleeping soundly on a flat calm morning and took a skin biopsy from it with a dart. The whale, greatly surprised out of its slumber, dove rapidly, breached twice, then moved a hundred meters away and went back to sleep (yes, I felt guilty).

Annoy a whale and it may exhibit a different kind of breach by hurling its back end out of the water to one side. This 'tail breach' usually seems to be a sign of vexation, and I've seen it not only directed at people but also from a mother whale when she wants to keep a misbehaving calf in line.

I find most curious the instances where a lone humpback will execute a long series of these high-energy behaviors. I have personally counted more than 150 consecutive breaches in a single session – with a lot of tail breaches, flipper slaps and tail lobs thrown in – from a single whale, which remained in more or less the same spot the entire time. I've seen such amazingly protracted displays many times, and always on a feeding ground. Occasionally, if I waited long enough to see the display end, the whale concerned would defecate, then stop and move on. Is endlessly repeated breaching sometimes about digestion or even constipation? I don't know, but it's an interesting thought!

Years ago, the researcher Hal Whitehead observed that breaching was far more common among the fatter whales like humpbacks and right whales than in the faster, sleeker species such as blues and fins. Whether this a coincidence is not clear; but given that slower whales are much more likely to be infested with external parasites (simply because it is easier for them to attach themselves), the difference may provide a clue to one of the functions of breaching. Perhaps it sometimes serves as a way of ridding themselves of external 'hangers-on'. Certainly the bodies of humpback whales (and right and gray whales) carry considerably more of this sort of baggage; blue whales, fin whales and their close relatives have skin that is much 'cleaner'.

Breaching is not the only acrobatic behavior among humpback whales. They will often slam their tails or flippers down on the surface repeatedly, and it's not clear what function this serves; again, 'lobtailing' and 'flippering' probably have different meanings depending on location, time of year, and social context. In the winter on a breeding ground, it's possible that such behaviors, when performed by a female, serve to call in

A breaching whale off Maui, Hawaii. Most species of whales breach, but none more so than the humpback – a trait which caused Herman Melville to write in his novel *Moby Dick* that 'He is the most gamesome and light-hearted of all the whales.'

'Lobtailing' involves the whale slamming its huge tail onto the surface, usually repeatedly. Like breaching, it probably serves multiple functions.

males. This is speculative, of course, but on occasion one sees an adult female joined by a young male, and it's not out of the question that the female uses flippering or lobtailing in an attempt to attract older males to displace her would-be suitor. This solicitation behavior happens in some other species, including elephants. In the West Indies, I have occasionally seen a female slap a young male with her tail, presumably because she didn't want to be harassed by the humpback equivalent of an annoying and over-sexed teenager who was on the prowl for a date.

Of course, whales aren't this energetic all the time. Particularly on calm days, you can often find a humpback whale floating motionless at the surface, apparently asleep. This is observed much more commonly in the higher latitudes of the feeding grounds than in winter breeding areas, almost certainly because it's simply too hot in the tropics for a whale to lounge around at the surface. In winter, we see whales go on much longer dives: 15-20 minutes is common, and humpbacks can even dive for up to 40 minutes in extreme cases. Underwater observations show that on many of these dives whales are sitting at or near the bottom, apparently resting.

But how does a whale sleep? Unlike us land animals, whales can't turn the business of breathing over to an automated system because they're divers who spend most of their lives underwater. They need control of their respiration, and as a result they've evolved to be voluntary breathers. However, this creates a problem.

How do you make the decision to breathe when your brain is asleep? It's very likely that humpback whales do the same thing that dolphins do, which is to rest half of their brains – one hemisphere – at a time. Presumably this keeps one half relatively alert to keep the animal breathing. Whales, it seems, can be quite literally half asleep.

Much has been written, and even more has been wildly speculated, about the intelligence of cetaceans. Many people, including some devotees of New Age philosophy, credit whales and dolphins with remarkable powers of intelligence, wisdom and gentleness. Sad to say that this is probably mostly just wishful thinking.

As we've seen, humpbacks are far from gentle with each other at certain times; the many scars and injuries carried by adult males bear witness to their frequent combat over females during the winter. Bottlenose dolphins – the infamous Flipper of marine parks

Intelligence in whales and other animals is difficult to define. However, humpbacks show sometimes remarkable complexity in their behaviors, from bubble-feeding techniques to the apparent cultural transmission involved in song.

everywhere – have been documented attacking each other as well as beating up and sometimes even killing small porpoises, evidently just for sport. Killer whales will often use seals as training aids to teach their young how to catch prey; I once watched juvenile killer whales practicing the art of slapping a harbor seal with their tails (not very successfully, it must be said) for a couple of hours before one of the mothers in the group intervened and put the poor seal out of its misery.

Yet there are certainly signs of a creative intelligence among some species. Dolphins in captivity not only perform quite complex tricks, but, more revealingly, can be taught linguistic and abstract concepts, and show a remarkable ability to discriminate between different objects. I would argue that humpback whales are tool users like ourselves. While they may not modify objects in their environment, their creation of unique bubble structures to catch fish – a process which involves complex co-ordination among individuals and a rigid ordering of actions – is judged to be truly a remarkable phenomenon by anyone lucky enough to have witnessed it.

After more than 30 years of working with humpback whales, I can say only this. As in humans, intelligence varies a lot among individuals: some whales seem a lot smarter than others. We see this manifest in various ways, perhaps most obviously in the creative variations that some individuals seem to develop in their bubble-feeding techniques, and in their apparent ability to learn such skills from others.

Approach a whale – especially a protective mother with a calf – in a small boat and you'll get an idea of how clever (or not) some whales can be. Unless you approach very slowly and at an even pace, whales will usually turn away and dive, leaving you to wait until their next surfacing to try again to get that elusive photograph or biopsy sample. Experience teaches you that you can sometimes fool an animal by, for example, running up ahead of it and shutting off the engine; if you're lucky and you judge right, the whale, not realizing you're still there, will come up near you. But on various occasions I have seen individual humpbacks figure this out and change their behavior accordingly. I remember one mother on Silver Bank in the West Indies who fell for each of our little tricks just once, and then never again. After a frustrating 45 minutes of this aquatic game of hide and seek, I eventually gave up and let her be.

Humpback whales are not Einsteins, but it's important to realize that they have evolved in a radically different environment to ours, as our measures of intelligence depend heavily upon our own physical and cultural frames of reference. Humpback whales and other cetaceans have survived for millions of years, and they are remarkable creations of Nature; they don't need to be loaded with the idle romantic baggage that we humans seem sometimes to want to project onto the natural world. When all is said and done, humpbacks are remarkably adapted to survive and prosper in an aquatic realm of which we still know remarkably little. Prosper, that is, if our own species does not destroy their food, their habitats, or the whales themselves.

Which brings us to a long and dark chapter in the history of the human relationship with humpbacks and other whales.

The eye of a whale is adapted for seeing underwater, and whales may be near-sighted in air. Because visibility is often poor in the ocean, humpback whales probably rely more on sound than on vision.

A Merciless Pursuit

Tucked away in a sheltered cove on the Aleutian island of Akutan is a collection of old machinery, rusted and ruined by decades of exposure to the unforgiving Alaskan weather. The wind whistles through old storage tanks, and boilers which long since ceased to function lie among the overgrown grasses. On the shore, an old wooden pier juts into the water, its barnacle-encrusted pilings eroded and askew. Today, there is nothing here beneath the bleak hills but these remnants of the past, serenaded only by the sound of wind, waves and the occasional bird call. But a century ago this place was a hive of activity.

This was once the whaling station of Akutan, which operated from 1912 to 1937. During that time, catcher boats fitted with harpoon cannons on their bows ventured out into the choppy waters of the Aleutian Islands, and each working day they would bring back the carcasses of whales to be processed. Blue whales, fin whales, humpbacks and even the occasional right whale were hauled up a slipway and methodically butchered, the blubber cooked in the boilers and rendered into valuable oil.

The bones of these giants can still be found in the shallows below what is left of the whaling station. A few years ago, I and my research team spent a few hours at Akutan, and recovered half a dozen rib bones which we sent for analysis to Diana Weber, then at the American Museum of Natural History in New York. Despite the fact that they had been lying in the water for decades, these old bones successfully yielded their DNA, which revealed what they had once been: mostly blue whales, and one fin. Amazingly enough, with modern genetic technology, dead men – and dead whales – do tell tales.

I returned to Akutan in 2007 and found more bones. As I stood there gazing at the ruins of the whaling station (beset by a thin drizzle which seems to be ubiquitous in this part of the world, even in what passes for summer), I thought of the animals that once had roamed and fed in these waters; especially the blue whales,

A humpback whale dives in the waters of Frederick Sound, Southeast Alaska. There, and in other locations on the coast of Alaska, whales were hunted from shore whaling stations established in the early 20th century. The frequent proximity of humpbacks to the coast made them an easy target for such enterprises.

which were so over-exploited by whaling that they have been completely wiped out from this area and are no longer seen here. Similarly, the entire population of the right whale in the eastern North Pacific is believed to number in just the tens of animals. However, Akutan's part in that depletion was minor – the near-extirpation of the right whale is part of a much more insidious story of illegal whaling by the former USSR.

Humpbacks were killed at Akutan too, but fortunately their story has a happier ending. Take a ship along the stunningly beautiful Aleutian Island chain today and you will often find an abundance of humpback whales. Scores of humpbacks gather here each summer to feed in the richly productive waters of the Bering Sea, feasting mainly on krill for several months before they begin the long migration to the tropics.

With a few exceptions, humpback whale populations worldwide have shown great resilience in their recovery from whaling. This is all the more remarkable in light of the fact that in many places in the 20th century, well over 95 per cent of the population was destroyed. Their destruction occurred at the climax of a long and bloody history of exploitation of whales and other marine mammals by humans.

The ultimate origins of whaling are lost in a distant and murky past. There are indications that the Phoenicians were hunting whales in the Mediterranean in ancient times, although whether these hunts were occasional and opportunistic or a true industry is unknown. We know from remarkable Bronze Age pictographs outside the city of Ulsan in South Korea that men conducted systematic hunts of whales several thousand years ago. The pictographs are so detailed that one can recognize individual species of whales in them, including rorquals that may well have been humpbacks. Among native Arctic peoples (the Inuit), whaling has been a central part of their culture for millennia. Indeed, the Alaskan Eskimo are so associated with the hunting of bowhead whales that they are known as the 'People of the Ice Whale', and remain so today.

The first known whaling enterprise that was organized for commercial profit occurred in the Bay of Biscay region of Western Europe, no later than the year 1070. There, coastal towns in northern Spain and southwestern France hunted right whales on a regular basis. The right whale takes its name from the fact that it was

The acrobatic and often dramatic nature of some humpback whale behaviors unfortunately made the species highly visible to whalers over distances of several miles, allowing them to more easily locate concentrations of the whales to hunt.

considered the 'right whale' to kill; it was slow and relatively easy to catch, and it floated when dead. For the early whalers, limited by the technology of medieval times to hunting from small boats powered by oars or sails, these were key advantages. They could rarely catch the fast rorquals such as fin or blue whales, and even if they had managed to kill one, the body would sink and thus could probably never be retrieved for butchering. With right whales, the carcass could be easily towed to shore and cut up on a beach. In addition, the thick blubber layer of a right whale (which can be up to 30 cm deep), when boiled, yielded a particularly rich oil which was used for lighting lamps. We know from medieval commercial records that the meat of right whales was also sold in the markets of coastal towns; in the 12th century the King of France levied a tax on the tongues of right whales – evidently the tongue was considered a delicacy for some medieval people.

Right whales were gradually reduced in number by the Biscay fishery, which exacerbated the situation by often taking mothers with calves, thus removing the prime reproductive portion of the population. By the 16th century, Basque whalers, who were renowned throughout Europe as the masters of this craft, had already crossed the Atlantic to whale in the New World. Basque whaling camps have been found throughout much of the coast of Labrador, and date back to at least 1530. Until recently, it was thought that both right and bowhead whales were taken in this region in more or less equal numbers, but genetic analysis of bones from these whaling sites has shown that it was primarily a bowhead fishery. This is interesting, because bowheads are today only rarely found so far south. The Basques conducted their hunts at a time when the climate was colder – the 16th century was in the middle of what has been called the Little Ice Age – and thus the distribution of the bowhead whale was shifted to the south of where this 'ice whale' exists today.

First Europeans, then Americans, were the pioneers of commercial whaling. After the New World was settled in the 17th century, small local whaling operations sprang up in various places along the eastern coast from the Carolinas to Nova Scotia. The late 18th century saw the beginning of a huge expansion of whaling away from the coast and into other oceans. This was led by ports in New England, notably New Bedford and Nantucket. Although several species were of commercial interest to these 'Yankee' whalers, much of the industry was

A mother and calf swim through tropical waters. Whalers would often kill a calf first, knowing that the mother was unlikely to abandon it, thus making harpooning her much easier.

A humpback 'chin breaching'
in Hervey Bay, Queensland.
Humpbacks were the main target
of shore whaling stations that
operated on both the eastern
and western coasts of Australia
until they were forced to close
for lack of whales in 1962.

focused on the sperm whale, which yielded the highest quality oil. New England whalers pursued long voyages of up to four or even five years' duration, and they ventured into the most distant and remote parts of the ocean in pursuit of the great sperm whale.

Right whales, too, were highly prized, and by the 19th century were far more plentiful in the Southern Hemisphere and the North Pacific than in the North Atlantic, where they had long been depleted by European and American colonial whaling. In 1835 the French whaler *Gange* arrived in the Gulf of Alaska (which became known as the 'Northwest Ground') and reported seeing 'a million whales'. This was hardly accurate, but it was certainly a reflection of the abundance of right whales in these waters. Other ships rushed to the area, and just fourteen years later right whales were so depleted here and in the nearby Bering Sea that many whalers gave up the right whale fishery to push into the forbidding waters north of the Bering Strait and hunt bowhead whales. Bowheads live among Arctic ice, and conditions were often perilous; indeed, some whalers became trapped in the ice at the end of the brief Arctic summer, and in 1871 virtually the entire American fleet was lost to such an entrapment. Nonetheless, if the conditions could be borne and survived, the profits were huge – at least initially.

Bowheads yielded high-quality oil, and their baleen, the longest of any whale at up to almost five meters, was much sought-after. The flexibility of baleen allowed it to be fashioned into a bizarre variety of products,

including buggy whips and umbrella slats; however, its principal use for many years was in the stays of women's corsets and the hoops of their skirts, two features that for some time were all the rage in European and American capitals. In other words, the demise of both the bowhead and the right whale (which also has long baleen) were driven at least partially by high fashion.

As elsewhere, the large stocks of bowheads in the western Arctic were quickly depleted, a fact which caused considerable hardship for the native Eskimo whalers of Alaska; hunting for subsistence and in an entirely sustainable manner (as they still do today), they had depended upon the ice whale for generations. Commercial whalers saw no reason to consider this in their insatiable greed for profit.

Two humpback whales engage in simultaneous flipper slapping in Hervey Bay, which is today an important stopover for humpbacks migrating south back to their Antarctic feeding grounds, and a mecca for commercial whale-watching.

Breaching together, a mother and calf leap from the water. Calves presumably learn some of their behaviors by imitating their mothers and other whales.

For centuries, whaling had been limited by the technology of the day. Early shore processing stations could hunt only locally until the development of ocean-going sailing ships, and even then these vessels mostly processed the whales that they killed at 'tryworks' (boilers for rendering blubber into oil) on shore. The invention in the late 18th century of an on-board tryworks allowed whalers to process their catch at sea, and suddenly the hunt for Leviathan became a global enterprise.

The great age of sail-based whaling saw whalers spread out across most of the world. Everywhere the same pattern was repeated: they wiped out the whales and then moved on, and by the late 1800s most of the populations of huntable whales had been discovered and exploited. What was needed was new technology, and new whaling grounds.

The former came to pass in the second half of the 19th century, with two inventions. The first, the steamship, provided the whalers with a means to hunt the fast, sleek rorquals that beforehand had been largely out of their reach. The second, the explosive harpoon, suddenly provided the hunters with a much more effective method of dispatching the whales. A harpoon fired from a gun – and later, from a cannon mounted on the bow – could kill a whale from some distance; no more did whalers have to endure long chases fraught with the danger of getting up alongside the animal, and trying to subdue it with hand-thrown harpoons. The new harpoons soon came with an additional feature: an explosive charge in the tip that detonated on impact and killed or severely wounded the animal.

Two men were behind this revolutionary invention. One, an American named Thomas Welcome Roys, was never quite as successful as the other, a Norwegian sealer called Svend Føyn. It was Føyn who meticulously worked out the details of the explosive harpoon and put it into regular commercial use, and for this he is widely regarded as the father of modern whaling. Roys enjoyed some success, and certainly had a knack for advertising: when an accident with his new invention resulted in him losing an arm, advertisements for his new product touted that it was 'so simple, you can use it with one hand'! With this technology, the stage was set for an expansion of whaling from which no whale was safe. The huge blue and fin whales, which until now had been largely immune to the hunt, suddenly became fair game. Then, in 1904 another event occurred which truly ushered in the modern whaling age, and guaranteed a slaughter on an unimaginable scale: the discovery of the vast, untouched stocks of whales in the Antarctic.

In 1900, the waters of Antarctic were largely unexplored. The Antarctic continent had reputedly been glimpsed by earlier explorers (including, possibly, James Cook), and was independently discovered at about

Whaling rules forbade killing calves or lactating females, but this was often ignored by whalers.

the same time in late January 1820 by a Russian expedition and an American sealing vessel. Whalers, long occupied by stocks of whales in better-known and less forbidding waters, had not ventured into this uncharted realm at the bottom of the world.

In 1902 that changed. A Norwegian whaler named Carl Anton Larsen sailed to the sub-Antarctic island of South Georgia, found huge numbers of whales, and reported in awe, 'I see them in hundreds and thousands.' In particular, blue whales – the most valuable of all – were highly abundant at South Georgia and in adjacent waters. Because baleen whales in the Southern Hemisphere are usually somewhat larger than those north of the equator, this included the largest animals ever to have lived on Earth: a female blue whale killed in this area in 1912 measured (depending on which statistic one believes), either 107 ft (32.6 m) or 110 ft (33.5 m) in length.

Two years later, in December 1904, Larsen and 60 other Norwegians had completed the construction of a whaling station at Grytviken on South Georgia, and modern whaling in the Southern Ocean officially began. Larsen caught 184 whales in his first year of operation, but the totals were soon to rise dramatically. Not surprisingly, other whalers followed Larsen's lead to these remote but astonishingly productive waters.

About this time, the commercial basis for the whaling industry was undergoing a major shift. Baleen was about to be replaced by the invention of plastic, and the discovery of petroleum meant that whale oil was no longer the most economical basis for lighting. However, the oil suddenly *could* be used in human food. In 1903, a process known as hydrogenation was invented which turned oils into solid, edible fat, and by 1914 whale oil was being thus converted on a large-scale. Remarkably, the unparalleled slaughter of whales that occurred in the 20th century was driven in part by margarine.

The introduction in the 1920s of factory ships freed whalers from their dependence upon land processing stations and allowed them to roam the seas at will, with steam-powered catcher boats bringing an endless supply of carcasses back to the factory ship for processing.

It is not clear how many whales existed in the Southern Ocean at the time whalers first began the hunt in 1904, but we can get some idea of their extraordinary abundance from the catch totals. The numbers are

Slow and relatively easy to catch, humpbacks were frequently one of the first species to be targeted – and depleted – by new whaling operations, especially those in coastal waters.

quite staggering. In the eight decades following Larsen's discovery, whalers killed 360,000 blue whales,
an astonishing 725,000 fin whales, 200,000 humpbacks, 200,000 sei whales, 400,000 sperm whales, and
130,000 animals of other species. In all, more than two million whales were slaughtered in the Southern
Hemisphere in the 20th century. In terms of sheer biomass, it was by far the largest slaughter ever conducted
by human beings.

Throughout the history of whaling, humpback whales were often regarded as second-class citizens in terms of
their commercial value. They were always a poor second to right and bowhead whales, with their long baleen
and huge reserves of oil-rich blubber, and to sperm whales, with the great prize of spermaceti locked inside
their great heads. Nonetheless, humpbacks were frequently the first target for any new land-based whaling
operation. The species has two characteristics that made it easy prey for early whalers: it is often coastal in its
distribution, and it is relatively slow, and therefore easy to overtake and kill. Humpbacks were less popular than
some other whales because they yielded a much lower quantity and quality of oil. Still, they were commercially
valuable and thus were the frequent focus of emerging coastal hunts. As long as the profit to be derived from
the oil was greater than the cost of obtaining it, the humpback whale was worth pursuing.

Many 19th-century Yankee whalers from New England made their fortunes on right, bowhead and sperm
whales, and many would bypass humpback whales because they had no wish to take up valuable storage space
below decks with the oil of a 'lesser' whale. Yet a few specialized in 'humpbacking', perhaps because, for a
while, it did not require arduous multi-year voyages to the ends of the Earth. Some whalers, notably those from
the town of Provincetown, Massachusetts, set sail in autumn for the humpback's breeding grounds in the West
Indies and, after passing the winter in the balmy Caribbean, they either returned home or spent the remainder
of the year chasing sperm whales in the low latitudes of the North Atlantic.

After the advent of modern-style whaling, shore stations were established in many locations – Akutan among
them. Steam-powered catchers preyed upon whales in nearby waters; they could not range beyond a distance

The curiosity of humpback whales
towards humans is manifest in
their close approaches to boats,
a behavior that was often fatal
in the days of whaling.

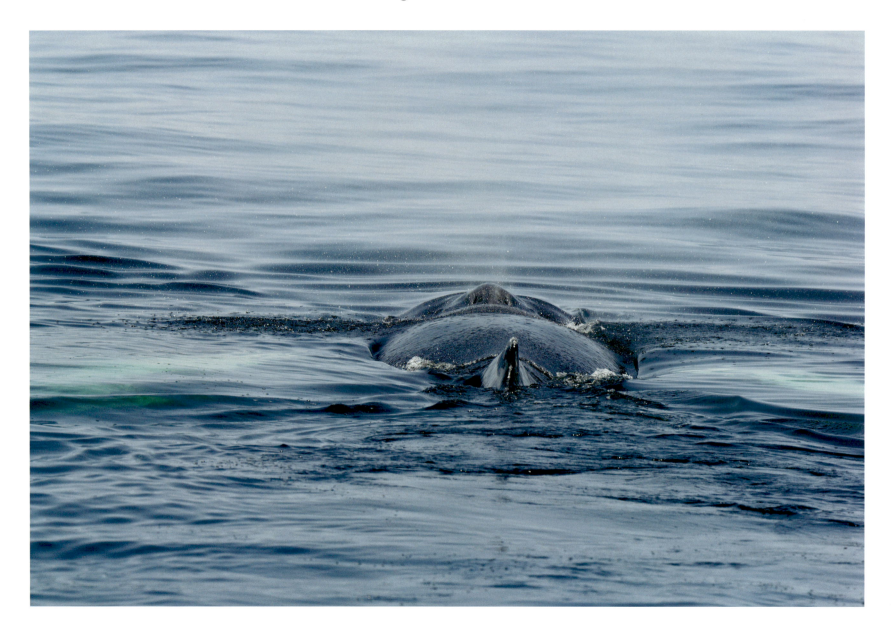

at which a carcass would spoil during the time it took to tow it back to the station. Given that humpback whale populations were frequently found feeding close to land, this made them an easy and obvious target.

Usually, it did not take long for the population to be depleted or even wiped out, at which point the whalers moved on to other species, if they were available. The case of two shore whaling stations in California in the 1920s illustrates the point. Whaling operations were opened at the towns of Trinidad and Moss Landing in 1919 and 1920, respectively, and they immediately began to exploit the abundant humpback whales that were found feeding off the northern California coast. Catches peaked at 502 whales in 1922, then gradually declined.

By 1926, the fishery was exhausted, the humpbacks were gone, and the whalers moved on to sei whales before the lack of any whales forced the two stations to close. Overall, more than 2,000 humpbacks were killed at Moss Landing and Trinidad; today, the population in the area is estimated to be perhaps 1,000 whales. More than 80 years later, humpbacks off California have still not recovered from whaling.

This same sad story was repeated over and over again in places as far apart as arctic Norway and Brazil. In many cases, the local extirpation of the population was hastened by the fact that other whaling operations were at the same time killing humpbacks at the other end of their migratory range. For example, an early 20th-century coastal fishery off Finnmark in northern Norway followed substantial catches of humpbacks in both the southeastern Caribbean and the Cape Verde Islands, both of which are now known to be breeding areas for the Norwegian whales.

Humpbacks could temporarily escape whalers by diving deeply, but they were usually easy to find again and then chased at the surface, until the exhausted whale would subsequently be harpooned.

Similarly, whaling in breeding areas off Brazil exacerbated an already bad situation created by huge catches made at South Georgia. Indeed, South Georgia stands as one of a number of examples of areas where a whale population appears to have been entirely extirpated. The speed with which the humpbacks' extirpation at South Georgia was accomplished was remarkable. Carl Anton Larsen's whaling operation at Grytviken killed their first humpback whale in December 1904, and by 1914 the whalers from South Georgia had killed an astonishing 21,894 humpback whales, virtually destroying the population. Although humpback whales were killed in small numbers until 1955 (the largest catch was one of 238 whales in the 1945/46 season), the population never recovered from this initial devastating assault.

The situation with blue whales in this part of the Southern Ocean was very similar. The total catch of blue whales there between 1909 and 1962 was 41,026, of which 39,296 were taken prior to 1936.

Like many species, populations of humpbacks were reduced by whaling by more than 90 per cent of their original size in some areas.

Astonishingly, in several years more than 3,000 blue whales were killed in a single season, with the highest catch being of 3,689 animals in 1926/27. Today, despite an apparent abundance of krill, the waters in which Carl Anton Larsen reported seeing blue and humpback whales 'in hundreds and thousands' now have virtually none. It is possible that the whalers did their job so thoroughly that they literally wiped out the whales' cultural memory of the existence of this rich feeding ground.

This phenomenon of whaling wiping out whales, with no recovery evident for many years, has occurred in a number of locations worldwide. Other examples include fin whales off Gibraltar, blue whales off Japan, humpbacks off New Zealand, and right whales in the eastern North Atlantic. In some cases, such as right whales in the Bay of Biscay, where commercial whaling had its beginnings, several hundred years have now passed without any evidence of the whales' return. If nothing else, whalers cannot be accused of not doing a thorough job.

Of all the innumerable operations that have made up the long history of commercial whaling over the centuries, none was more efficient nor more ruthless than that of the former USSR. And no species paid a greater price in that tragic story than the humpback whale.

In late October of 1966, an imposing ship steamed quietly through the placid waters of the Suez Canal. Clad in drab industrial gray, and flying a Soviet hammer and sickle flag at her masthead, the vessel was accompanied by a large fleet of smaller craft. Any observer able to decipher Cyrillic script could have read, in rusting metallic letters on her bow, the name *Sovetskaya Ukraina*. The more experienced would perhaps have identified her as a whaling factory ship, traveling with her attendant fleet of catcher boats and scouting vessels on a transit that would take them south into the Red Sea and beyond.

Although the whaling fleet may have presented a noteworthy sight, *Sovetskaya Ukraina*'s passage through the Canal was nothing unusual. As far as anyone knew, she was bound once more for the great whaling grounds of the Antarctic, and was simply taking the shortest route there from her home port of Odessa on the Black Sea.

A few days later, however, as the fleet entered the Gulf of Aden, it abruptly broke its southbound track. Unmarked by anyone except some local fishermen, *Sovetskaya Ukraina* and her catchers turned to the northeast. As they cruised within sight of the desert coastline of Oman, the fleet fanned out. On November 4th, they began to kill whales.

A whaling fleet engaged in the practice of whaling is hardly cause for comment. What made these catches unusual, however, was that almost all of them were illegal.

A mother and calf head to the surface to take a breath.

155

Over the next two weeks, the vessels of the Soviet fleet swept the northwestern Indian Ocean. Their search for whales took them from Oman to the Gulf of Kutch off Pakistan, through offshore waters west of the Indian city of Bombay, and south to the Maldive Islands. By the time *Sovetskaya Ukraina* finally resumed her course for the Antarctic on November 21st, her catcher boats had delivered more than 300 whales to the huge floating factory for processing. Most of the animals had been either humpbacks or blue whales, two species that were officially considered 'protected' under the international regulations that governed commercial whaling at that time.

When the Soviet fleet reached the Antarctic, the pattern was repeated. Already-depleted and supposedly protected stocks of whales were plundered for several months until the onset of the austral winter. Finally, as the weather turned increasingly foul, the factory ship and her catchers began the long journey home.

In keeping with its obligations as a signatory to international whaling agreements, the Soviet government dutifully reported that the *Sovetskaya Ukraina* fleet had taken a total of 2,727 whales during the 1966/67 season, all of them 'legal' species such as sperm, fin and sei whales. The actual catch was 5,127 – a difference of 2,400 whales. Nor was *Sovetskaya Ukraina* operating alone. Elsewhere, two other Soviet factory fleets had taken a further 5,323 animals that went unreported. In a single season, 7,723 whales had literally disappeared without a trace.

This flagrant disregard for international agreement, and for the declining status of Antarctic whale stocks, was no renegade act of piracy by the commanders of the fleets concerned. The illegal catches of that whaling season were simply the latest in a carefully planned official strategy that had been implemented almost 20 years before. Few people suspected it, but the Soviet Union had been plundering the world's whale populations with abandon since 1947. By the time that the illegal catches

Nowhere was whaling conducted more intensively than in Antarctic waters.

finally ended in 1973, the Soviets had killed over 180,000 more whales than they had officially reported. In the process, they had probably succeeded in dooming at least one population of whales to extinction.

In addition to the 'official' record of catches that was submitted to the International Whaling Commission, the Soviets also maintained a second log. These secret logs gave the true catch data for each expedition, and many years later they were to prove instrumental in setting the record straight. Several Soviet biologists kept their own records of the true catches, often at personal risk within the Soviet system; it is only because of their foresight that many of the catch records has now been corrected, although major gaps remain for some areas and years.

During her 1966/67 season, *Sovetskaya Ukraina* worked in the northern Indian Ocean, where they killed 238 humpback whales in just 10 days. The hunt was extraordinarily efficient, and ruthless. *Sovetskaya Ukraina* and her sister ship *Sovetskaya Rossiya* were the largest whaling factories ever built, and each had more catchers than any other factory ship – up to 25. All the catchers would fan out into a long line, so that each boat was just within sight of the one on either side of it. When a catcher found something, everyone would converge on the spot, kill every animal in the area, then move on.

In 1965, an Australian scientist named Graeme Chittleborough published a scientific paper summarizing extensive studies of two of the major humpback whale populations in the Southern Hemisphere. Using his data to estimate mortality rates, Chittleborough observed that known catches of humpbacks were insufficient to account for the very high rates suggested by his calculations. After considering various possibilities, he concluded that the only reasonable explanation was that someone was taking large numbers of humpbacks illegally.

Surprisingly, no one at the International Whaling Commission pursued Chittleborough's accusations. When the truth was finally revealed, even Graeme Chittleborough was staggered by the scale of the illegal catches on humpbacks, which had been hit more heavily than any other species. Over the years, the Soviets

Humpback whales were among the hardest hit by illegal Soviet whaling. Some 25,000 were killed in just two Antarctic seasons, resulting in a population crash and the closure of shore whaling stations in Australia and New Zealand.

had reported taking 2,710 humpback whales in the waters of the Southern Hemisphere. The real total was more than 48,000. Of these, almost 25,000 were killed in just two seasons (1959/60 and 1960/61) in the waters south of Australia and New Zealand. Most were taken by two factory fleets under the command of the most notorious whaling commander of all, a man named Alexei Solyanik. And most were in part wasted, each whale's blubber stripped by powerful machinery in just 15-20 minutes and sent into the huge boilers to be rendered into oil. The rest of the carcass was often thrown back into the ocean.

These huge catches of humpback whales caused an almost immediate population crash. Until 1961, shore-based whaling stations on the eastern and western coasts of Australia had been easily meeting their quotas of several hundred humpbacks per season; but after the Soviet catches south of this region, whales suddenly became scarce, and the stations were forced to close for lack of whales. The same pattern was repeated at a shore whaling operation run by the Perano family in New Zealand.

Twenty-eight years after Chittleborough's paper, in December 1993, Alexey Yablokov stood before a large group of marine mammal biologists at a conference in Galveston, Texas. Addressing the meeting's concluding banquet, he stunned his audience by revealing that the Soviets had engaged in massive illegal whaling for three decades. Yablokov, a respected biologist with a long history of research on whales, was then the Science Advisor to Russian President Boris Yeltsin. His speech was made possible only by the dissolution of the Soviet Union four years before.

Thus emerged the truth about Soviet whaling. Recognizing the importance of setting the record straight, the American scientist Bob Brownell immediately began working with Yablokov to identify sources for the true catch data. Although Yablokov was the one to finally break the silence, most of the details were furnished by other former Soviet whale biologists who had all witnessed the illegal catches first-hand from the decks of factory ships. Encouraged by Yablokov, they began work in various parts of the now-fractured Soviet empire to unearth the true catch data.

Whales such as humpbacks were killed for oil, rendered by boiling their thick blubber, and sometimes also for meat and bonemeal.

Today, almost all of the Southern Hemisphere catch records have been corrected and published. In addition, the Russian scientist Yulia Ivashchenko is analyzing new information on takes in the Northern Hemisphere. Although the magnitude of these catches is smaller, the Soviets were far from idle north of the equator. In all, we estimate that the unreported catches numbered about 180,000 animals worldwide, and they included several protected species. Almost half were of humpback whales; but blue whales, sperm whales, sei whales, Bryde's whales, bowhead whales and right whales were all killed in large numbers. Everything that crossed the bow of a catcher boat was taken: any species, and any size, from young calves to the oldest animals. In keeping with the spirit of the best communist philosophy, the Soviets did not discriminate.

Although some populations seem to have rebounded from the over-exploitation to which they were subject by the USSR and other nations, one population that may not is that of the right whale in the eastern North Pacific. Right whales in the Northern Hemisphere are indisputably among the rarest of all the world's whales. By 1900, right whales were already so rare throughout their range that they had ceased to be a principal target for whalers anywhere. Like their Southern Hemisphere counterparts, they were completely protected from hunting by international agreement in 1935.

A few years ago, Bob Brownell and I undertook a review of all records of right whales in the North Pacific this century. The exercise revealed an alarming trend. Although right whales have never been numerous in the eastern part of this ocean during the 20th century, reasonable numbers were being sighted for many years. Whale catchers searching for other species reported seeing modest concentrations of right whales each year, particularly in the Bering Sea, the Aleutian Islands and the Gulf of Alaska. Around 1964, however, a dramatic drop in sightings is evident. Despite the fact that the search effort actually increased, there were barely 80 observations of right whales in the entire eastern North Pacific from 1964 to 2000.

In light of what we now know, it was not hard to guess the nature of the calamity that overtook the right whale population in the early sixties. Nor is it difficult to interpret a large number of right whale 'sightings' reported by Soviet whalers around this period. There, as elsewhere, the whalers went beyond mere observation

A rainbow appears briefly in a whale's blow. The blow has always been a burden to whales in the sense that it is highly visible and thus made it easy for whalers to spot them from miles away.

of these animals and killed as many as they could, with disastrous consequences. We now know that the Soviets killed more than 500 right whales in the Gulf of Alaska and the Bering Sea; this was probably the bulk of the remaining population, and the catch consisted of many large, reproductively mature animals.

Less than two centuries after the whaling ship *Gange* reported seeing so many right whales in the Gulf of Alaska, the species is now so rarely sighted in the region that a single observation is noteworthy enough to merit publication in a scientific journal. A recent abundance estimate by Paul Wade, myself and colleagues put the population at just 30 animals, and while that is probably on the low side, it is not likely to be a huge underestimate. We cannot be sure, but it is entirely possible that when the few remaining right whales in the eastern North Pacific live out their lives and die, the species will be gone forever from these waters. Although Soviet whalers were certainly not responsible for the bulk of the catches on this population, they may well possess the dubious distinction of having effectively finished it off.

The North Pacific right whale, as well as the 25,000 humpbacks killed in the Antarctic in just two years, represented two of the more dramatic examples of what happens when international agreements fail to include provisions for adequate oversight. Given the opportunity, humans will always cheat; and humpback whales have frequently paid the price.

Today, one can stand on the hills at Akutan in the Aleutians and see humpback whales within a few miles of the coast, feeding on abundant krill. On occasion, they are so numerous that their blows make up a ghostly forest in the chill air. As the SPLASH project has found, humpbacks have made a remarkable recovery from whaling in the North Pacific, despite humans' attempts to wipe them out.

But you can stand on those same hills for weeks and you will very likely never see a blue whale. Eight hundred and thirty-five of these giants were killed here, a testament to their former abundance. Yet today, the great blue whales are merely a memory, and we are left to contemplate their bones in the shallows of Akutan, a silent reminder of the dangerous power of human greed.

Three humpback whales dive together in Frederick Sound, Southeast Alaska. The tendency of humpbacks to aggregate in sometimes large numbers in high-latitude summering areas characterized by abundant food resources, inevitably made killing them much easier for whalers.

Winged Leviathan

By the end of World War II, it had become clear to even the most reluctant whalers that some sort of quota system was needed to prevent the commercial extinction of the world's whales. In 1946, the whaling nations signed the International Convention for the Regulation of Whaling. The Convention created the International Whaling Commission, a body which met annually to oversee research on whale populations and to set scientifically based quotas that would theoretically balance the industry's revenues with the need for long-term conservation of populations.

Not unpredictably, a process that was conceived as a necessarily good idea quickly fell victim to the desire for profit. Since whales are difficult to study, it was virtually impossible to obtain indisputable proof to support predictions of population crashes. There was frequently doubt, and its benefit was never awarded to the whales. During the 1950s, the whalers continued to slaughter their quarry in record numbers. In just 10 years, more than a quarter of a million fin whales were killed in the Southern Ocean, together with tens of thousands of other whales.

By the end of the decade, virtually all objective scientists recognized that many whale populations were being exploited well beyond the limits of reason. Over the next few years, as catches declined and some populations received complete protection from hunting, it became clear that the International Whaling Commission's intention to oversee management based upon sustainable exploitation had fallen short of reality. And as we have seen, the USSR's campaign of illegal whaling was secretly ensuring that this shortfall was considerably greater than anyone could have imagined.

The history of whaling is a textbook example of how humans mismanage a resource. When the resource is abundant, everyone gets into the business. But when the resource has declined from over-exploitation,

Happily, humpback whales are now making a strong comeback in many places, although few if any populations have reached their pre-whaling numbers.

the industry still has a great deal of money tied up in the business – ships, crews and other expensive items – and this over-capitalization provides a strong incentive to deny that any problem exists. John Gulland, a British fisheries biologist, once said it best: 'Fisheries management is interminable debate about the condition of fish stocks until all doubt is removed. And so are all the fish.' This perfectly sums up 20th-century whaling.

In 1982, however, the International Whaling Commission passed a moratorium on commercial whaling. This represented a huge victory for anti-whaling nations and conservation organizations that had worked towards this moment for many years, ever since the rise of the environmental movement in the 1960s. Organizations such as Greenpeace raised awareness among the public, as much of the world began to shift its view of the planet and its conspicuously finite resources. Indeed, whales became a symbol of the plight of the Earth, and the Save the Whales movement was led in part by countries such as the United States, the United Kingdom and Australia – countries that had formerly been major players in the business of whaling.

Nonetheless, whaling today is far from dead. Japan, Norway and Iceland continue to catch whales of various species in the North Atlantic, North Pacific and Antarctic, and all three countries (and their allies at the IWC) continue to press for the overturning of the moratorium. This will not be easy to achieve, for under IWC rules a three-quarters majority vote would be required, and the organization is currently more or less equally split between pro- and anti-whaling members. There are also serious concerns regarding the inspection system that would have to accompany any return to commercial hunting. The whaling nations maintain that the existing system is adequate; others point to the past Soviet illegal whaling as the prime example of why complete transparency is necessary. It is noteworthy that although the IWC's introduction

Although whaling continues today, humpbacks are not currently the target of commercial hunts.

in 1972 of an International Observer Scheme was supposed to eliminate cheating by placing inspectors from other countries on factory ships, we now know that this was far from foolproof. Indeed, Soviet illegal catches continued, in the presence of inspectors from Japan – to which the USSR happened to be selling whale meat at the time.

While the whaling nations work towards the lifting of the moratorium, two large loopholes in the International Convention for the Regulation of Whaling allow these three countries to continue their hunts. Norway and Iceland both utilized a clause in the Convention which allows any member nation to 'object' to a decision, and thus not be bound by it. Japan takes advantage of another provision, which permits members to issue permits to their nationals for the killing of whales for

scientific research. This clause made sense when the Convention was signed in 1946, because at that time the only way to study whales was to kill them. However, it was never envisioned as a means to circumvent a ban on whaling, and since the IWC moratorium came into effect in 1986, Japan has used this loophole to kill more than 12,000 whales – six times more than all the 'scientific' catches of all nations combined from 1952 to 1986.

The 'science' practiced by Japan has little relevance to the management of whale populations, and today there is virtually nothing of substance you can learn from a dead whale that cannot be obtained using one of the many available non-lethal techniques.

Humpbacks are still killed in a few native fisheries in Greenland, and off the Caribbean island of St Vincent. In Greenland, the local Inuit were recently allowed to resume the hunting of humpback whales, the taking of which was banned by the IWC in 1986.

Whales in Prince William Sound, Alaska, site of the infamous Exxon Valdez oil spill in 1989. Catastrophic oil spills can harm whales from poisoning, inhalation of toxic fumes, and the clogging of their baleen.

Japan's primary argument for scientific whaling generally revolves around a need to better understand the role of whales in the ecosystem, a need which Japan claims can be studied only by killing whales. These advocates for a resumption of commercial whaling use the global consumption of fish by whales as an argument for why whales should be killed (the oft-used euphemism is that they must be 'managed'). Surely (the argument goes) they are out-competing human fisheries and other, unrecovered, whales for food, and so must have their populations reduced to restore the balance. Consequently, Japan must kill whales to learn what and how much they are eating, and to study the way they interact with each other. The fact that the great majority of whales in the Antarctic eat krill – something that has been known for over a century – and that sophisticated non-lethal studies by Ari Friedlaender and colleagues have strongly suggested that Antarctic humpback and minke whales exploit different ecological niches and thus aren't in competition, doesn't change the Japanese argument one iota. The sad reality is that Japan decided what the results of its research were going to be long before the first 'research' whaling ship ever left port.

At the International Whaling Commission's Scientific Committee, I have watched over the years as Japan has shifted its rationale for whaling in sometimes creatively contorted ways. In the 1990s, Japan's argument was that minke whales had to be killed because they were out-competing now-rare blue whales and thus suppressing the latter species' recovery. Never mind that there was no evidence for such competition, or that killing even a few thousand of the numerous minke whales in the Antarctic would not make the slightest difference even if competition did exist. Then some years ago new estimates of minke whale abundance showed a decline of several hundred thousand animals in ten years. This presented Japan with a huge problem, because there were really only two explanations for the decline: either it was real and minke whales were in trouble, or the surveys which had produced these estimates were unreliable. Remarkably, Japan concocted a third alternative which recast the minke whale – once the villain and persecutor of blue whales – as the victim of supposedly burgeoning populations of humpback whales. Now suddenly humpbacks were the guilty party, out-competing the poor minkes and driving them into the Antarctic ice where the surveys could no longer count them – hence the decline in numbers. If this sort of spurious logic was presented in a high school science paper it would likely be graded with an F, but at the IWC it is frequently given the same weight as more rational arguments in meeting reports.

Looked at objectively, there are several major flaws in the competition argument. First, the sizes of many whale populations today are at a small fraction of their levels in pre-whaling times when commercial fish populations were considerably larger and much healthier than they are today. Second, the primary predators of fish are not whales, but other fish. Third, the removal of top predators (such as cetaceans) can cause major ecosystem perturbations, with consequences for human fisheries that are actually negative. And finally – the most obvious point – human over-fishing (not whales) is the cause of the precipitous decline of commercial fish stocks worldwide.

So yes, whales eat a lot, but the ocean was apparently doing just fine, with far more whales in it than we have today, before we came along and 'managed' it.

Currently, whaling presents little threat to humpback whales. At present, there are only two known humpback

Overfishing by humans – not whales – is the main cause of declining fish stocks today.

175

hunts in the world, both conducted by native peoples, and both in the North Atlantic. A possible third hunt, by the inhabitants of the remote island of Pagalu off the coast of Equatorial Guinea, was active in the 1980s, but no one seems to know whether it continues today.

Far to the northwest on the other side of the Atlantic, a hunt for humpbacks occurs off Greenland by the native Inuit people. The killing of humpbacks there was banned by the IWC in 1986 because of concerns about the small size of the population, but in 2010 the Commission considered that the population had recovered well enough to allow some hunting to resume. This has been a rather controversial issue, because of claims that the hunt is not entirely 'subsistence', and that some of the meat from whales killed off Greenland ends up in supermarkets and restaurants as far away as Copenhagen.

Down in the humpbacks' breeding grounds, men from the small island of Bequia (part of St Vincent and the Grenadines) in the southeastern Caribbean have pursued an annual hunt for humpbacks since 1876, when the islanders were taught the business of whaling by a Yankee whaling ship from Provincetown, Massachusetts. Until recently the hunt was conducted with largely traditional methods, including two rather lovely traditional sailing craft whose design could have come straight from the pages of Herman Melville's *Moby Dick*. The International Whaling Commission gives Bequia a quota of 20 whales over five years, although it is unusual for this number to be reached. One complication is that the Bequia fishery has traditionally preferred the easier-to-kill mothers and calves; despite being explicitly prohibited by the rules of the IWC, calves are often the victims still, but no penalty is ever levied against the whalers for these infractions. Nonetheless, it is very unlikely that the small Bequia hunt has any impact on the North Atlantic population, which as far as we can tell has continued to increase in size in recent decades.

Indeed, our winged whale is, by and large, doing well despite all our efforts over the centuries to extirpate it. Many populations of humpback whales were reduced by over 90 per cent of their original numbers by commercial whaling. Nonetheless, the humpback is, it seems, a resilient species. Most populations that are

A newborn calf seeks protection under the head of its mother. Mothers and calves are at risk from local hunters off the Caribbean island of St Vincent, whose ancestors learned how to catch humpbacks from 19th-century New England whalers.

under study are growing steadily, and a few may be gradually approaching the size they were at before the onset of whaling. Reported rates of population growth vary from around three per cent a year to almost 12 per cent; the latter figure is pretty much the maximum rate of increase of which the species is capable, constrained as it inevitably is by biological limits to reproduction.

In the North Atlantic, the population was last estimated (in 1992) at about 11,000, and is probably a good bit higher than that today. A large international collaborative study in the North Pacific (the SPLASH project mentioned previously) recently estimated that there are more than 20,000 humpbacks in that ocean. South of the equator, there is evidence of strong growth in humpback whale populations everywhere from Brazil to Australia.

The exceptions, however, are significant. The Arabian Sea population – the one that, unlike any other, remains in warm waters year-round – may number as few as 100 animals, and faces considerable threats to its existence from fishing gear entanglements, as well as from shipping and pollution in a part of the world heavily dominated by the production and transport of oil. Across the world, the vast watery realm of Oceania has perhaps 3,000 humpbacks today, but far more were there before whaling, and the reason for their slow recovery in the South Pacific remains unclear. In the 1950s, a scientist named Bill Dawbin conducted surveys at Fiji, logging a couple of hundred humpback whales a week in this winter breeding ground; Dave Paton duplicated Dawbin's survey methods in recent years, and found a handful of whales. The effects of the huge Antarctic catches made by the USSR in 1959-61 are still apparent in this region, even 50 years later.

Perhaps most strikingly, at South Georgia in the South Atlantic – where Antarctic whaling really had its beginning in 1904, and where thousands of humpbacks were killed – it is uncommon to see a humpback whale today. Whether this is because the population was so completely destroyed that no cultural memory remains of the existence of this habitat, or because of some other reason, is unknown. But the seas around South Georgia, which once teemed with humpback and blue whales, are strangely empty of them now. Perhaps this will change as Antarctic humpback whale populations grow and seek out new feeding grounds in future years.

A humpback breaches in the Sea of Cortez, Mexico. Whalers began killing humpback and gray whales off Baja California in the 19th century. Today, here and elsewhere, such animals are the targets of whale-watching expeditions.

How many humpback whales exist in the world today? We're not sure. Counting whales is notoriously difficult. Humpbacks are one of the most accessible species for researchers because much of the time they live close to coastlines, and individual whales are easily identifiable by natural markings or through genetic typing of small skin biopsies. We can estimate the abundance of whales using a number of methods, each of which has its own advantages and problems. Running a ship or an aircraft through whale areas and counting the number of animals seen is one way; identifying individuals is another. But in both cases the method is only as good as the regions that your surveys manage to cover; if there are lots of whales outside your study area, then they won't be counted. Not to mention the fact that whales are creatures of the deep, and surface only occasionally to breathe; this means that they're often not visible when your survey passes through, and you

Because whales spend most of their lives underwater and are found in remote and inhospitable offshore habitats, conducting even a simple count of their numbers is fraught with difficulty.

have to account for that in your subsequent analysis of the survey data.

That said, we have pretty good numbers (we think) on several populations of humpbacks worldwide. Scientific estimates or rough guesses would today put the North Atlantic population at around 15-20,000 whales, the North Pacific at 20,000, and the various Southern Hemisphere populations collectively at perhaps 50,000. So today there are maybe 100,000 humpback whales in the world – though that is a very approximate number, and it could be in error by a substantial percentage.

One hundred thousand is not a small figure, but it is certainly well below the number of humpback whales that existed before the first harpoon was thrown at this species some centuries ago. More than 200,000 humpbacks were killed in the Antarctic in the 20th century alone. Some rather controversial genetic analysis by Joe Roman and colleagues suggests that the pre-whaling, pristine population was in the hundreds of thousands, and perhaps it was. We know only that the humpback whale was greatly reduced by the protracted depredations of humans.

While whaling is, for the time being at least, no longer much of a threat, other human activities are. The number one killer of humpback whales today – together with countless other cetaceans – is entanglement in fishing gear. Long lines of lobster pots or crab traps, endless miles of gill nets, and a few other types of fishing equipment present a hazard to whales that in some areas is effectively a minefield, so dense is the concentration of gear. Sail a boat along the coast of Maine, for example, and you will encounter innumerable

lobster traps, each one representing a hazard to any diving whale. Research by Jooke Robbins and David Mattila on identified individuals from the Gulf of Maine – my old study population – indicates that more than 70 per cent of whales show scars from previous encounters with fishing gear, and that perhaps more than 10 per cent are entangled annually. While whales survive many of these encounters, those unfortunate enough to sustain a particularly bad entanglement can suffer protracted deaths from starvation or disease.

Many humpback whales swimming free today owe their lives to scientists. Researchers from the Gulf of Maine and elsewhere maintain whale rescue operations which attempt to free humpbacks and other whales

In some areas with a high density of fishing gear, most of the humpback whales in a population will come into contact with nets or lines at some point during their lives.

Diving whales often do not see ropes or nets in the water column until it is too late. While many whales break free of such entrapments, some carry fishing gear with them for months or even years.

from entanglements. This is not easy, but they often employ an old method from the days of historical whaling. 'Kegging' is a technique in which a line is clipped to the entangling gear, and large buoyant plastic floats are attached to the line. This slows the whale down, and also makes it much easier to relocate every time it dives. Eventually, whales often give up and allow the rescuers to cut them free using a variety of custom knives and other specialized tools.

This activity is inherently dangerous, as one would expect when dealing with distressed 30-ton animals. Humpback whales are usually quite tractable, but right whales – which are very powerful animals that can be quite aggressive under threat – are another matter altogether, and these days the rescue teams do not attempt to disentangle a right whale unless the animal has first been sedated. Delivering a dose of sedative of the appropriate strength, through many inches of blubber into the muscle of a moving and panicked large whale, has required some extraordinary creativity on the part of Michael Moore and a team of engineers at Woods Hole Oceanographic Institution in Massachusetts, but this remarkable operation has been successfully attempted several times in recent years.

Another possible threat to humpback whales is pollution. We know little about the effects on whales of the vast stores of industrial chemicals that have been discarded, flushed or otherwise found their way into the world's oceans, but samples taken of the tissues of humpback and other whales show persistent levels of toxins

such as DDT, PCBs and flame retardants – and these are just the ones scientists routinely test for. Although the humpback's position on the food chain generally results in them accumulating less of a toxin burden than most toothed whales, the potential impact of such chemicals is worrying. Laboratory studies have shown profound effects on reproduction and survival in other mammals.

Thanks to the grand system of circulation among ocean currents and the atmosphere, human pollutants are found all over the globe, including in the most remote places imaginable. Roger Payne and Iain Kerr of Ocean Alliance sailed around the world to conduct a global survey in which they took biopsy samples from sperm whales; they found contaminants everywhere, including in the deep ocean far from land. Levels vary, certainly:

The winged leviathan off Maui, Hawaii. There is good evidence that Hawaii was not a habitat for humpbacks until relatively recently, but today whales occupy the island waters in their thousands during winter.

humpback whales off California show higher levels of (for example) DDT than humpbacks off Alaska. But nowhere can you find a whale whose tissue is unmarked by the pernicious poisons that our industries churn out.

Entanglement and pollution are not the only threat faced by cetaceans today. Humpbacks and other whales are also hit by ships, as ever-increasing maritime commerce comes into conflict with cetacean habitats. One of the places where this is certain to become an acute problem in the future is the Arctic. As sea ice disappears through climate change, previously inaccessible areas will open up and for the first time in history provide regular ice-free routes from Europe to Asia and the Americas, across the top of the world. The massive increase in noise and pollution that will result will likely be the most devastating environmental change that Arctic cetaceans have ever seen. And the effect will not be confined to the Arctic: for example, when the Northern Sea Route and the Northwest Passage open up, the volume of shipping through the now relatively quiet Bering Sea will drastically increase as vessels transit the narrow Bering Strait and travel through passes in the Aleutian Islands en route to or from the Pacific.

The effects that our society's uncontrolled industrialization has wrought upon the world's climate will have huge impacts on the ocean. A warmer world may see humpback whales pushing further towards the poles to colonize new habitats as the waters in the highest latitudes become increasingly free of ice; but whether such an expansion of their range will represent a benefit to the whales, or simply create confusion and a disruption of their existing migratory cycle, is unclear.

Humpback whales have been here for several million years. During that time they have certainly had to deal with major climatic shifts, notably through periodic cycles of shrinking and expanding habitats as ice ages came and went. These beautiful winged leviathans have survived huge changes throughout their history on our planet. They have made their long migrations year after year, century after century, and have continued to fill the oceans with their haunting songs for uncounted millennia, through thick and thin.

Now, let us hope that they can survive us.

Ever adaptable, humpbacks seem to be a resilient species that has come back from the devastation wrought on their populations by commercial whaling. Today, the whales face new challenges in a rapidly changing world.

Humpback Whale Distribution

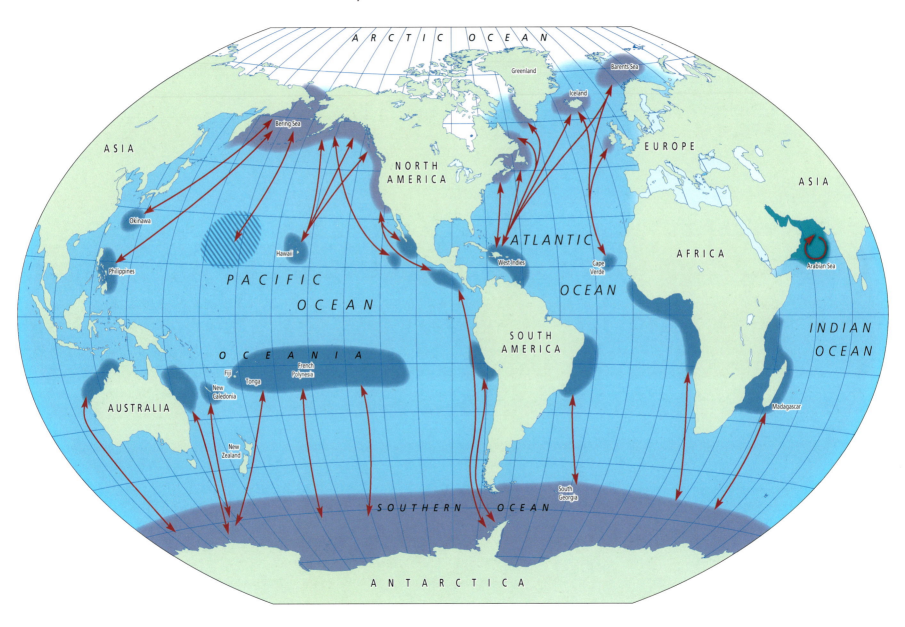

Humpback Whale Facts

Scientific name:	*Megaptera novaeangliae* ('Big wing of New England')
Average length (adult female):	13 m (43 feet)
(adult male):	12.5 m (41 feet)
(newborn calf):	4.3 m (14 feet)
Average adult weight (female):	25-30 tons
Breadth of tail:	4.6 m (15 feet)
Length of pectoral fin:	4 m (13 feet)
Longevity:	uncertain, probably 50-80 years

Distribution – Humpback whales are among the most widely distributed of all the large whales, and are found in all the world's oceans, from the equator to polar waters. With the exception of the Arabian Sea (where whales remain year-round), humpback whales from all populations make long seasonal migrations from summer feeding grounds in temperate or high latitudes to winter breeding and calving areas in tropical waters. In extreme cases, these migrations may exceed 4,500 nautical miles in length.

Feeding – Humpbacks are 'generalists', and unlike some other baleen whales feed on a variety of prey. Commonly eaten species include small schooling fish such as herring, capelin and sand lance, as well as a small shrimp-like crustacean known as krill. Antarctic populations feed largely on krill, while the diet of Northern Hemisphere humpbacks is often more varied. Humpbacks are known to produce huge nets or clouds of bubbles to trap prey, notably schools of small fish.

Reproduction – Both males and females attain sexual maturity between five and ten years of age, although males may not actively breed until later. The gestation period is approximately 11.5 months. Females give birth to a single calf on average every two to three years, although consecutive-year calving is possible. Calves leave their mothers after a year of nursing.

Current status – Because not all populations are currently under study, worldwide abundance is not known. There are an estimated 15-20,000 humpbacks in the North Atlantic, 20,000 in the North Pacific, and perhaps another 50,000 in the Southern Hemisphere. Some populations are large and growing strongly, while in a few others recovery appears to be slow or absent.

Acknowledgments

Phil Clapham

Conducting research on large animals who insist on living in environments that are inhospitable or downright dangerous to humans isn't exactly the easiest undertaking in the world. Consequently, it usually involves co-operation and collaboration with colleagues. I consider myself very fortunate to have worked over the years with a wide variety of people who are sufficiently insane to want to get into a boat with me, and who have contributed greatly to our knowledge of humpback and other whales. Along the way, most of them have become good friends, and all have been companions at sea who have shared with me endless days characterized by cold, fog, gales, engine breakdowns, unco-operative whales and other privations and tribulations – as well as innumerable moments of excitement and beauty in between.

Among these many individuals are Charles 'Stormy' Mayo, who gave me my start in the field way back in the Dark Ages (1980); the ever-affable dons of North Atlantic whale work, David Mattila and Steve Katona; Scott Kraus, Roz Rolland, Amy Knowlton, Marilyn Marx, Philip Hamilton, Moe Brown and the other fine folks at the New England Aquarium (despite their unaccountable preference for right whales); Nan Hauser, Rochelle Constantine, Debbie Steel, Scott Baker, Claire Garrigue, Michael Poole, Mike Donoghue, Olive Andrews and the other members of the family that we call the South Pacific Whale Research Consortium.

Also (in no particular order), Karen Steuer, Sharon Young, Desray Reeb, Bob Brownell, Dave Wiley, Rich Sears, Jooke Robbins, Erin Falcone, Suzanne Yin, Oswaldo Vasquez, Mason Weinrich, Carole Carlson, Tony Martinez, Amy Kennedy, Brenda Rone, Alex Zerbini, Irene Seipt, Irene Briga, Harriet Corbett, Bill Amos, Fred Wenzel, Bruce Mate, Jim Mead, Charley Potter, Dmitry Tormosov, Randy Reeves; and the late Al and Aaron Avellar, who introduced whale-watching to the east coast of North America, and set the standard thereafter.

Finally, I owe an unpayable debt to my extraordinary wife, my other heart, Yulia Ivashchenko. I never imagined that working with the person you're married to could be so effortless, and so much fun.

Acknowledgments

Colin Baxter

My first sight of Humpback Whales was almost 20 years ago, off the coast of Massachusetts on a whale-watching boat trip with my young family. We were enthralled, how could anyone not be, seeing such large animals so close and full of life, right there in front of us and yet totally free in their vast ocean world stretching way beyond the horizon. Then the boat had to leave and get back to port to collect the next group of enthusiastic day-trippers. The whales rapidly became distant black shapes before being lost from sight and the whole experience suddenly felt very brief. So we went back again, and again, and again before flying home across that very same ocean.

There is something about whale-watching that is at first contagious, and then most definitely addictive, and so ever since the early 1990s we have taken every opportunity to just keep watching whales, and of course for me to photograph them too.

The pictures here are very much a personal collection, gleaned from countless outings on boats of all shapes and sizes, along with some photographs taken from the shore. The boats have all been either regular commercial whale-watching trips or private charters, and it is to the captains and crew of all these vessels that I am most grateful. Their knowledge, skill and respect for the whales have allowed me and fellow passengers to witness these special moments. My sincere thanks to you all. In Provincetown, Massachusetts, the many captains and crew of the Dolphin Fleet. On Maui, Hawaii, a variety of whale-watching operators out of Lahaina and Maalaea. In Alaska we had such a good time exploring the endless beauty of sheltered inlets and sounds admidst

magnificent scenery. A special thank you to Scott and Julie Hursey of the *Heron* out of Petersburg, Southeast Alaska and to Murray and Phyllis Tate of the *Nuliaq* out of Valdez, Prince William Sound. On the waters surrounding Baja California, Mexico the knowledge and expertise of Mike Keating of the *Spirit of Adventure* out of San Diego, led to so many terrific whale encounters above water. In Hervey Bay, Queensland, Australia, the captains and crew of the many whale-watching operators we had such fun with.

Swimming with whales for the first time can be a life-changing experience, and it definitely has been for me. A very big thank you to Roger and Erika Maier, of the *Bottom Time II* out of Fort Lauderdale, Florida, who first encouraged us to travel out to Silver Bank, north of the Dominican Republic, and witness humpback whales in their world beneath the surface.

It is further south, in the waters among the islands of Vava'u, Tonga where my humpback whale encounters have been the most amazing and most memorable. My thanks to Christy Butterfield of the *Melinda*, for introducing us to this gorgeous part of the world and to the whales that visit there. Above all though I will always be indebted to Allan Bowe and his family and crew on Mounu Island, Vava'u – a paradise among whales. Allan's knowledge and experience of humpback whales has been invaluable to my quest in achieving much of this imagery, and his ability to 'place' us in the water so skillfully, close to the whales yet with the utmost consideration and regard for their behavior is exemplary. Thank you very much indeed. Watching whales is indeed addictive, so I expect we will return!

Index

Published in Great Britain in 2013 by Colin Baxter Photography Ltd, Grantown-on-Spey, Moray, PH26 3TA, Scotland

www.colinbaxter.co.uk

Text © Phil Clapham 2013   Photographs © Colin Baxter 2013
Copyright © Colin Baxter Photography Ltd 2013

ISBN 978-1-84107-577-8   Printed in China